M000119784

Penny's From Heaven

Penny's From Heaven: Stories of Healing

BY PATSY SWENDSON

LANGMARC
PUBLISHING
AUSTIN, TEXAS

Penny's From Heaven:
Stories of Healing
by Patsy Swendson

Cover Design: Michael Qualben
Cover Photographs: Robert McLeroy
Illustrations: Aundrea Hernandez

Published by
LangMarc Publishing
P.O. Box 90488
Austin, Texas 78709-0488
www.langmarc.com

Library of Congress Control Number: 2006927574

ISBN: 1-880292-831

DEDICATION

Today I shudder at how I once judged people long before the birth of my daughter, death of my parents, loss of love, death of two college roommates, divorce, serious depression, devastating betrayal, death of a dream, loss of myself from control and manipulation, and loss of what I had thought were very dear friends.

Long before my life really began, one day at a time.

I don't have all the answers. People are all human, just as I am. They hurt, they cry, they grieve, they fight to find happiness and sometimes in the process, others are hurt.

But I have found that being present while the hearts and souls and tremendous struggles of Penny's patients are revealed, I say, "There but for the grace of God." I began to count my incredible blessings. My struggle now is to ease their pain, if only for a moment.

This book is for my friends, good friends, best friends, dearly-loved friends who spent the night with me to "make sure I was okay." Friends who listened endlessly and willingly took on my pain, which I had unknowingly foisted upon them, exhausting them.

A friend who called me every morning at 7:00 A.M. to make certain I got through the night. And there were friends who fed me and read to me. Friends who made me leave my house, kicking and screaming, to go to dinner or a movie. The best friends of all, who just simply sat by my side.

And my resident pet friends, no matter what, were there and saw me at my worst. And the dear friends who took me to church and held me up and didn't care that I cried just walking into the sanctuary.

These friends all encouraged, supported, and loved me. Friends who a little at a time chiseled away the darkness until, just every once in a while, I could see a glimmer of light.

They are loved and cherished beyond words. They have been, and are, the singular most extraordinary relationships of my life.

And last and certainly not least, to my daughter, Kim, who is waiting in the wings with great love, respect for, and commitment to all living creatures.

It is to all of them that I dedicate this book with great love.

FOREWORD

Few dogs *really* possess it—the intrinsic ability to instantly convey a profound connection to an unfamiliar person. I call it "talent," and it is obvious that Penny is generously endowed. But more than nice visits occur at the rehabilitation hospital in which Penny volunteers. Beyond connecting with her patients, Penny becomes their catalyst for change. Her meet-and-greet role expands to one of a tender modality as she interacts with her patients. Each time a patient works to remember something about her, or speak to her, or moves a hand and arm to pet her, Penny facilitates success.

For many years, I have been intrigued by the creation of exercises that incorporate talented dogs into physical, occupational, and speech therapy. In 1993, at my first Delta Society conference in St. Louis, I sat fascinated as Shari Bernard, OTR, discussed her structured, goal-directed animal-assisted therapy program at Baylor Institute for Rehabilitation in Texas. During that same time period, I discovered a group in Chicago called Chenny Troupe, whose volunteer dog and handler teams worked as a group in addressing functional patient goals in a rehabilitation hospital.

Then in 1995, I landed my first professional contract with a rehabilitation hospital in Oklahoma City. During the nine years that followed, my own dogs and I worked as a team with therapists in an in-patient setting, developing and delivering games, exercises, and activities to address individual patient goals. I also developed seminars, books, and a DVD so that volunteers, educators, and health care professionals might learn to enhance clinical and educational goals through creative dog-related activities, too.

Perhaps it's because I am primarily a dog trainer that my focus during this time has been on developing dog-related activities through which patients can address clinical goals. I believe talented dogs serve as hooks and cause patients to become more receptive to working with their therapists. I like to think that talented dogs open doors that connect to our patients, and it's a real asset when therapists can more easily affect patient responses through interesting dog-related activities.

Until I read Patsy's stories, I was mostly interested in the "addressing goals" parts of my opening-doors metaphor. But soon I discovered that Patsy uses words to create vivid images of therapeutic doors and that she has a unique ability to capture the very moments when doors have cracked open. Through her stories I've gained a heightened sense of the door-opening moments in my own work—the moments when life-changing connections have occurred.

Certainly, *Penny's From Heaven* is about the power of a talented therapy dog to influence patient behavior within a rehabilitation hospital. This is a delightful book that highlights the powerful gift of one very special dog to quietly transform human lives; but I believe the ultimate achievement of this book is its affirmation of human compassion, strength, and grace. Readers of this book might be surprised at Patsy's insight into the human spirit. *Penny's From Heaven* contains remarkable word-pictures of human connection—to Penny, to each other, and to self.

Readers will probably appreciate *Penny's From Heaven* in different ways. In addition to a great cover-to-cover read, it serves me well as a book of daily meditations. I feel this book is the antidote for every therapy dog handler who has felt discouraged or wondered "why?" at some point, and it is an excellent resource for promoting discussion among health care professionals who include dogs in any way in therapeutic environments.

Skilled handlers might especially enjoy the author's quiet partnership with her dog, as I did. Patsy's focus and maturity as a therapy dog handler and her deep reverence for each patient are ever present. She writes, "And then I remember this isn't about me...or even Penny. It is about the moments. What does matter is that they happened."

In capturing and sharing the moments, Patsy reminds each of us "what does matter." Her vehicles for delivering her messages are powerful, brief stories that I feel will establish a place for her among distinguished writers. Each time one of her stories opens a door for you, I hope you'll venture through and discover something of yourself inside.

Kris Butler
American Dog Obedience Center, LLC
Norman, Oklahoma
Author of *Therapy Dogs Today* and
Therapy Dogs: Compassionate Modalities
www.DogPrograms.com

PREFACE
OUR HISTORY

I had been on the CBS affiliate in South Texas for twenty years. I had produced and hosted my own daily cooking show and in the process written forty-nine cookbooks. The crew at the station lovingly called me the "fluff queen." No hard-core news here.

In addition to the cooking shows, personal appearances, and all the perceived glitz that accompanied it, (as well as a lot of calories), I produced and hosted most pet-related features and several worldwide travel features. But my heart and true passion came alive whenever I was sharing the camera with a four-footed friend...and sometimes a three-footed one.

I hosted and produced and agonized through twenty years with an "Adopt a Pet" program, which aired live on the 5:00 P.M. newscast. We would feature a homeless critter, three-legged dogs, blind or deaf dogs, puppies, cats and kittens, senior animals with no place to live out the rest of their lives, and we even featured an occasional abused horse. With each one I fell in love. I did everything in my power to find them an appropriate home, one where they would be respected, cared for, and loved. A home where the human companion animal bond would be a deep and loving one.

Additionally, I did investigative reports on tormenting and painful cruelty issues, inhumane euthanasia practices, and more. But in the process I was fortunate enough to have met many wonderful people with similar interests, and hopefully I made a small difference.

Invited to become a charter member of the Delta Society of San Antonio, I ultimately served for three years as its president.

During this time I was truly blessed with Casey, a little mixed breed stray that lived with me twenty years and ten months. Casey became one of the first of two "Delta Dogs" in San Antonio.

During my years as president of Delta San Antonio, the chapter was instrumental in getting certified, health and temperament-tested animals visiting in 68 health care facilities in South Texas. For this I am extremely proud. The organization continues today in San Antonio.

It was an uphill battle convincing doctors and hospital administrators to let us bring our certified dogs into their facilities. But we did it! Our greatest challenge was getting our therapy dogs into a respiratory therapy hospital. But we did it! And we later formulated the first pet loss support system in South Texas in conjunction with the United Way. Today it is commonplace to see dogs and cats working their magic in long-term care facilities, as well as hospice facilities and schools.

Because of the Delta Society and the tutelage and enthusiasm of the late Professor Leo Bustad, a pioneer from Washington State University School of Veterinary Medicine, and his crusade to recognize and promote the positive link between pets and people, my passion took hold. It was then that the message from Anatole Frances began to make sense: "Until one has loved an animal, a part of one's soul remains unawakened."

What a tremendous opportunity being able to reach thousands on television. With this in mind, I produced and hosted a five-part series called *Creature Comforts*. This series focused on the human companion animal bond to include equine therapy for cerebral palsy patients, service dogs from California's Canine Companions for Independence working with severely handicapped individuals, pets and their benefits for the elderly and lonely, dolphin therapy in Florida, and pets and children.

The series won the Media Commendation Award from the national Delta Society, the Mark Francis Award from the American Veterinary Medical Association, and the Lynn Anderson Distinguished Service Award in Texas.

During this time I truly wanted to give back to a community that had supported me for so many years. So twelve years into my television career, I approached the Guide Dogs of Texas about lending my name and support to an annual benefit for their organization. The "Patsy Swendson Unbirthday Bash and Barn Dance" became a major fundraising event for eight years.

It was then that I fell hopelessly in love with golden retrievers. I followed their training at the foundation with relentless interest and celebrated as the first guide dog had an official placement.

I was on the speakers' bureau for the American Heart Association and Stroke Survivors of San Antonio about the benefits of pet-assisted therapy for heart patients and stroke survivors. I spoke to anyone who would listen. Standing in line at the supermarket to waiting in doctor's offices, anyone was a potential ear to my passion.

So I suppose it was meant to be when that "higher power" stepped in with just a simple phone call from the Executive Director of the Guide Dogs of Texas telling me they had a two-year-old golden retriever named Penny that had just been released from the guide dog training program. Was I interested in adopting her? Oh sure, I was interested, but I already had three dogs — Lulu, a Great Pyrenees rescue, my very old precious Casey who needed lots of attention and medical care, and Wally, a Lhasa apso rescue.

But what could it hurt to just meet her? I went to the guide dog offices, and I tried to remain aloof. "Well okay, just bring her by the house and let's see how she gets along with the other dogs."

And then, "Well, just let's try it overnight and see how it works."

It didn't take long until I found that Penny had a sweetness to her that is not easily put into words. I then looked over her paperwork and noticed that we shared the same birthday...we were both born on February 20th and obviously both Pisces. I was getting hooked.

Then very late her first night with me someone tried to break into my home, turning and jiggling the doorknob. This had never happened before and never since. Penny barked ferociously and frightened them away. I called the police, and they told me how fortunate I was to have such a fine dog. "You'd better be real glad you have her." The other three dogs slept through it. That did it, no doubt about it. Penny was my dog and a living source of great comfort. My life was never to be the same again.

The first few weeks it was as if a "diva" had entered my home. She had this "love me, love me" attitude. Everyone was posturing to see who was the "alpha." Penny's trainer told me she liked this certain kind of food, she enjoyed being combed rather than brushed daily, she preferred a lawn that is kept clean, and she would sleep by my bed. He neglected to tell me she was terrified of being separated from "her human" and she would only respond to very specific verbal and hand signals.

Since she was a few days old, Penny had been preparing to become a guide-dog-in-training and ultimately, a working guide dog. This meant 24/7 she was "with" her person. Penny had flown in airplanes, been to movies, restaurants, hotels, shops, anywhere a visually impaired person might need to be, and she would stay in the yard only as long as it took. Mediocrity was not in her vocabulary. I had to learn an entirely new language. Part of this learning taught me that Penny was well equipped to cheer the solitary soul, love life, and live it passionately. When she would go any place with me, the room would light up instantly.

More than once I questioned my ability to take on this responsibility. But the deep pleading brown eyes did it and seemed to tell me I could do it. So we began. I would walk into the garage and close the door, first for two or three minutes and work up to five minutes. She would become stressed and extremely agitated that she wasn't with me, but with diligent practice it very gradually became easier. Finally, I could actually leave the house! Now my girl is content with my disappearances up to eight hours. But if I am in the house, in my office or yard, she will not tolerate a door closed between us. I can live with that. She is like Velcro, but blessedly so. It doesn't feel right if she is not near me. This includes being under the dining table during meals, as she was trained to do for a visually impaired person and close by the shower in the bathroom.

I am reminded of a wonderful quote from an unknown author that goes something like this, "Goldens take your heart, and cherish it. They walk with it, and sleep with it, and they will never let it out of their sight. When it's their time, they will take a little piece of it with them to remember you by, and leave a piece for you to remember them by."

When Penny walked into my life, I knew she was different, something truly exceptional. What I didn't know was that she was essentially going to save my life in more ways than one. Because of her I will never be the same. She has changed my life and my goals. My faith has been renewed and my spirits have been lifted. The pieces of my life have been put back together even better than before. I am resilient. And now I know if I am knocked down again, I will embrace life, try again and succeed by faith. I see myself mended. I know now when you make the biggest mistake ever, something good, and perhaps even great, will come from it.

Sometimes I worry that to leap from that safe, knowledgeable place of writing cookbooks to writing this book is to put me in a place where I could be judged. My very stern English teacher in prep school in Oklahoma was judge, jury, and hangman to me. But I remember her, I learned from her, and now I thank her. With each lesson taught and absorbed, she managed to make me proud of my words and proud of what combinations of words could convey.

No cookbook this time. This time I will write for the sheer pleasure of it. There are stories to be told and things I need to say, must say. It isn't my goal to become a writer; I simply want to write.

Writing from the heart of things we know comes from intense listening and really hearing. I now have learned that not every word has to be a commitment. And I also know that what I do governs my life and quality of my life.

I want to share Penny's stories of healing and the stories of the people she touches and of those beautiful souls that love her.

Because of this uniquely gifted four-footed golden angel, I have learned to listen—*really* listen. I am a better person for the pain I have endured and learned from and most importantly survived. I have learned to be more compassionate, loving, and giving. I am working on being more nonjudgmental and loving unconditionally. These traits, I am learning from Penny.

My life is just beginning!

Here is my patchwork quilt of stories. I hope you feel warm and content as you wrap yourself in Penny's "snuggle therapy."

It is my deepest hope that you will meet my Penny in her stories with amazement and awe and that you, too, will be uplifted.

Patsy Swendson

"We write because something 'touches' us. We write because we want to 'touch' someone else. We write to 'get in touch' with the divine or because the divine has somehow 'gotten in touch' with us."
The Right to Write
—Julia Cameron

ABOUT THE ILLUSTRATOR

Aundrea Hernandez is an illustrator/designer with professional experience in creative direction of various media. She has been a senior graphic designer for several companies, including LangMarc Publishing. She designed eight of our beautiful book covers, and we were pleased to have her create her sensitive illustrations of Penny and the patients for *Penny's From Heaven.*

For more information about Aundrea's work, contact langmarc@ booksails.com.

ACKNOWLEDGMENTS

Acknowledging amazingly supportive people somehow seems less than sufficient. They have been insurmountably significant in my journey.

The courageous patients in HealthSouth and other healthcare facilities in which Penny and I have worked, I must salute first and foremost. I have been blessed and tremendously honored to have witnessed their tenacity, humor, challenges, and moments of intense grief, as well as overwhelming delight in taking tiny little steps.

John Lovitt, a former patient of Penny's, who would not take no for an answer, in a period of just one week took my manuscript and Penny's stories under his wing, picked up the phone and called his publisher to tell her about Penny and her remarkable, inspirational stories at HealthSouth Rehabilitation Institute of San Antonio.

Lois Qualben, LangMarc Publishing, for helping my dreams and passions become a reality and for paving the way for the rest of my life—words are not sufficient. Mike Qualben, for making Penny come alive in the book cover.

Vicki and Jack Stephens from the Skeeter Foundation for dedicating themselves selflessly to the Human Companion Animal Bond. Kris Butler for her unselfish support of a gal and her dog she has never met. Dan Earl, D.V.M. for taking such good care of Penny and all my dogs. Andy Anderson, D.V.M. for always being there. They are both truly everything veterinarians should be.

To beautiful red-haired, fair-skinned two-year-old Avalon Ann Marlin for reminding me what is truly important in this world. Susan Hearn at RIOSA for teaching Penny to find the treat under five paper cups and supporting every idea I have ever had.

Actress and author Betty White will always be an inspiration to the world with her warmth, humor, caring, and compassion. Well known and greatly loved for her work with Morris Animal Foundation and the Delta Society, Betty renews faith in all that is good in the world. For me, her endorsement of *Penny's From Heaven* is the ultimate affirmation.

Terry Hershey, with his love of his own golden Penny, inspired and supported every step taken by this Texas gal he's never met. Without Terry I'm not sure this book would have happened. He has truly been my "sacred necessity."

Mike Lingenfelter who knows the true blessing of what it means to have an "angel by his side."

Marty Becker, D.V.M. for knowing, believing, and understanding. Drs. Onghai, Zorrilla, and Thompson for recognizing and believing in the health benefits of pet assisted therapy.

Aundrea Hernandez, the world's best graphic artist, for bringing Penny so beautifully to life in her illustrations and capturing her soul.

Karen Haram and Rose Mary Budge from the *San Antonio Express News* for their magic with words and faith in Penny. Robert McLeroy for his expert photography and patience.

Jasmine Skala for training me, not the dogs. Stanton Smith for keeping my computer working and setting up Penny's web site. Loyce Balas for keeping my Bed & Breakfasts afloat so beautifully during the process.

Debra Baker from Guide Dogs of Texas for selling me this marvelous friend and therapist for one dollar. Rochelle Lesser for teaching the world the joys of golden retrievers.

And to HealthSouth RIOSA (Rehabilitation Institute of San Antonio) for opening their doors and letting Penny walk into this place of intentional healing with open arms.

EXPECTATIONS

I have been lead to realize that each and every time Penny and I enter the hospital we will experience amazing and awesome things.

Penny doesn't see what most people see, or even what I see. In this place where healing begins, she doesn't see a missing arm or leg or a scar. She pays no attention to age, physical disabilities, or emotional dysfunction. I believe that my best friend and I can do anything, or nothing, and healing will happen simply by the greatest gift of all, Penny's presence.

There are no substitutions for effort and commitment, nor for the things that Penny brings to other lives with her magical talent to communicate with people.

I have been, beyond a doubt, blessed to have had the opportunity to experience the truly magnificent and inspirational.

If we were to listen closely with our hearts, or set it to music, it would sound like love.

Intimacy
Distractions from pain
Feelings of loss supported
Visual tracking
Affection
Demonstrations of courage in the face of despair
Ability to solve problems
Self-awareness
Stress reduction
Socialization
Reminiscing
Memory
Posture
Endurance
Distraction

Range of motion
Laughter
Speech
Communication
Relaxation
Nurturing
Affection, giving and receiving
Confidence
Problem solving
Success

Find peace, health, wholeness, connection, and completion in the small miracles.

— Mohawk Onondaga Healer

PENNIES FROM HEAVEN

I found a penny today
   just laying on the ground
But it's not just a penny
   this little coin I've found...
Found pennies come from heaven
   that's what my Grandpa told me
He said angels toss them down
   oh, how I loved that story...
He said when an angel misses you
   they toss a penny down
Sometimes just to cheer you up
   make a smile out of your frown...
So don't pass by that penny
   when you're feeling blue
It may be a penny from heaven
   that an angel's tossed to you...

©1998 Charles Mashburn
With Permission

In the Beginning

I remember it as if it were yesterday, my first memory. I was barely four and had just proudly repeated a new word I had heard my father say. My mother went into a rage. The next thing I knew I had a bar of soap in my mouth and a "sound spanking," as they called it.

I had no idea what I had done wrong, only that the consequences were devastating. I ran sobbing hopelessly, as only a little girl can do, outside to Blackie, my cocker spaniel, and our hiding place.

I knew he would understand; I just knew it. He didn't let me down.

I buried my face, tears, and soapy mouth into his soft, precious fur and cried for what seemed like forever. When my tears finally dried, I didn't know much more about why I had been reprimanded, only that I felt better for having my Blackie to talk to, to love, and comfort me.

No judgment was issued. Blackie was very simply just there, loving me unconditionally.

This was the beginning!

A Gift From a Dog

I think of Penny not as a dog, but as a gift. A gift I am able to share with others, my most precious gift.

When my furry offering enters the rehab hospital and patients see her, whether for the first time or the tenth, they almost always remark how beautiful she is. And then the gift is truly revealed.

The patient's breathing frequently slows down and is steady. Their blood pressure often lowers. Many times their facial muscles relax and their eyes soften. The frowns, caused by pain and disillusionment, disappear and often their mind is momentarily without worry. More often than not their voices become softer and big smiles and shining eyes light up their faces.

They can feel the softness of Penny's fur, and in the process they whisper words to her I will never know.

It is often impossible not to become more relaxed in Penny's presence. The patients frequently become quieter. And for that moment they are only here—only now.

Our goals were achieved.

A golden gift.

PREPARATIONS

There is a lot more to preparing for a visit than simply putting a leash on Penny and getting in the car. Kris Butler in *Therapy Dogs Today: Their Gifts, Our Obligation* (Funpuddle Publishing Associates, 2004) says:

> "It simply can't happen without an energetic handler. The dog is not going to train himself, bathe himself, jump in the car and drive himself to a nearby school or hospital. Handlers participate in animal-enhanced programs because they benefit, too."

That is an understatement. Penny and I had been visiting for a year when I suddenly had the emotional props knocked out from under me.

During that time, visiting the rehab hospital was quite literally my only joy. Honestly it was quite a challenge to get Penny bathed and ready, much less to set aside my grief and put on a happy face to greet the patients. Some days I would cry all the way there and all the way home. But while I was there my complete and total focus was on Penny and the patients.

Looking back, it was unquestionably the best thing I could have done. I was trying with all my strength to courageously pull myself up with one arm, while extending the other arm to the patients. Blessedly, each week it became just a little easier.

You see, whether the patients knew it or not, we were both healing and making preparations for our futures.

Through it all, Penny was by both of our sides.

"True happiness is not attained through self-gratification, but through fidelity to a worthy purpose."
— Helen Keller

HER NAME IS PENNY

As I approach each patient, I say, "Her name is Penny. Would you like to visit with her?"

Sometimes I am asked, "What does she do? Does she do tricks?"

"She doesn't," I said. "She is a therapy dog. Her therapy duties include cuddling, nuzzling, being patient, and gently placing her head on laps. She also listens without falling asleep, is nonjudgmental, comforts, and loves unconditionally."

Penny does what she does best. What she gives, money can't buy!

She is an angel in disguise.

As patients touch her, many times I hear, "She is so soft isn't she?" Keen senses are reawakened.

Most of the time patients understand. Occasionally they don't.

One patient asked, "What is she going to be for Halloween?"

"A golden retriever," I said. The lady laughed and laughed.

She doesn't have to be anything but what she is. This very special dog leaves paw prints in so many hearts, as she opens people to joy, sorrow, comfort, and the many emotions and senses they have forgotten or had to set aside.

This is Penny's mission in life.

What Truly Matters

I had been on television twenty years. It forced me into the public eye. Everywhere I went, everything I did was watched. I had to wear the right thing, say the right thing, do the right thing. It was seldom that I was not the center of attention. I truly longed not to be recognized, to just be me.

During this time, I found when visiting healthcare facilities with Casey, my first therapy dog, the entire focus was on him. Who was on the other end of the leash did not matter in the slightest. I loved it. I could inhale deeply, relax, and enjoy. Casey, at least for a brief time, could take over as the center of attention. This pleased me on several levels.

But I was not entirely correct in my assumption of what was the most important part of the equation. As I have watched pet therapy teams work together for many years, there often appears to be a need for the owner to be recognized. And they want their dog recognized for the beautiful, intelligent animal that he is. That isn't necessarily wrong, but it is not what truly matters.

In reality, it isn't about the handler/owner or even the therapy pet.

It is solely about the patient. It isn't about me, and it isn't about Penny. Egos must be set aside. It is quite simply about that particular patient, at that particular moment, and his or her struggle to heal and improve their quality of life.

Sure Penny and I get our applause, but the honest motivation behind why people visit with their pets must be analyzed as to what truly matters. Only when it is accepted that the patient must come first will their work be completely successful. The patient is the true hero.

Maureen Fredrickson-McNamara, MSW, Executive Director MNlinc, stated it perfectly in her foreword to Kris Butler's wonderful book *Therapy Dogs Today: Their Gifts, Our Obligation.*

"Those handlers who understand that the accolades belong to the person struggling to heal and not to their dogs or themselves have reached a significant level of maturity and expertise in this work.

"Without this understanding, the handler remains in competition with the dog and the patient for reward and recognition."

She continues, "The work of a therapy dog is an intimate journey between the dog and the person they visit. Handlers must be prepared to witness such intimacy, give time for the expression of pain, support feelings of loss, and demonstrate courage in the face of rage and despair. In rooms where an addict battles withdrawal, a child struggles to walk, or a victim of sexual assault recalls past horrors, there is no place for the handler to ask if the person likes their dog. To work with a therapy dog is to assist people in the slow and personal task of healing."

A PLACE OF BELONGING

To some it may seem odd when I say that when I enter the hospital with Penny, I feel I am where I belong. Walking into the rehabilitation gym is often like Christmas morning. The smiles, the outstretched hands, the warm feelings of visits with close friends you've never met before give it a special atmosphere.

It is a place full of people I don't know and many I will never see again. The patients come and go and we, more than likely, will never know what happens to them.

But it is enough that we entered their lives, if only for a brief time.

My friends are busy with retirement and nurturing grandchildren.

Their faces light up with joy when they tell me about potty training, trips to the zoo, and holding that precious baby for the first time. Much like my face must light up when I tell them Penny's stories.

I can't change who I am, nor can I change the circumstances of my life. Sometimes it makes me sad, but to be instrumental in alleviating pain, changing a life, drying a tear, whether to a grandchild or someone you don't even know, is ultimately truly amazing.

For this place of belonging I am grateful and truly blessed.

EVERY SINGLE DAY

Every single day I whisper to Penny (as well as my other dogs) that I love them. I find great joy in their presence and a sense of peace. They, in return, ask nothing of me but to love them. Many of my human relationships have been guarded, about holding something back and not being totally who I am. And one was about the worst kind of betrayal.

Recovery has been slow. But I have found there is something miraculous and healing about loving my dogs. My love for them is unconditional. Their love for me is unwavering. When I have been so sad I didn't think I could go on, there they were, silently sitting beside me. Penny's head on my lap offered me a warmth and closeness that isn't judged or questioned. This love has helped me heal and is now helping others on their roads to healing as well.

With Penny, having been through guide dog training, I now find it ironic that she has become my guide dog. She has led me to a place I never imagined. A place I never knew existed. A place I have always yearned for.

With Penny, I am rewriting the script of my life.

Check-In

Penny has a routine on her weekly workday at the hospital. The night prior, I take out her red and tan monogrammed L.L. Bean™ canvas tote bag and set it in the rocking chair by the back door.

We check to make certain we have paper towels, plastic bags, antibacterial wipes, photos of Penny's roommates at home, photographs of Penny to give the patients, hospital ID tags (both hers and mine), water dish, and treats. Also included are Penny's hairbrush, a rubber KongBall,™ and a squeaky toy, all for the patients to work on manual dexterity.

As I lay out the leash on the dining room table and the tote bag gets filled, Penny's soft brown eyes watch closely. She knows, and she is ready.

The next morning, she gets a light breakfast, a last minute visit to the back yard, and a final thorough brushing. I check her ears, eyes, and feet and nails as I proudly "dress her" in her royal blue therapy dog vest and sometimes a special bandana. She waits at the door to the garage, wagging excitedly and incessantly. After jumping into the backseat, she settles down for the fifteen-minute ride. Rides are great!

We get to the hospital and search for just the right blade of grass (rain or shine) before checking in at the receptionist's desk. While I sign in, Penny wastes no time running around to the back of the desk and plopping her head into the lap of the receptionist. Guests and visitors, as well as arriving outpatients, all stand patiently waiting to pet her. Some respectfully ask permission. Penny approaches each one. No one is ever left out.

Some days it takes us ten to fifteen minutes just to get down the hall and say good morning to everyone.

As we turn corners, Penny sticks her nose into office doors to visit special friends before entering the rehab gym. They all "love on her" and laugh as she leaves each one a souvenir of dog hair from this loving "golden encounter."

I watch Penny closely as she "works the room." I see her spirit and soul and feel an incredibly deep love for her.

Funny—only a couple of weeks ago, someone told me that I "needed to get a life."

I am blessed. I have found my passion.

I wonder if they have.

A PERMANENT JOB

We have a routine. When Penny and I finish checking in, we go directly to the recreation therapy room. I give her a final brushing and a full water dish. This accomplished, Penny knows she is about to go to work. But there is one part of this morning routine that is non-negotiable.

Miss Cathy, a stroke survivor who volunteers her time, is always so happy to see Penny and give her a big hug and smile and ask her how she is.

Cathy's wardrobe has changed somewhat over the years we have been visiting. She now wears "puppy proof" slacks on "Penny's day." You see, each time Penny gets ready to begin "her rounds," she has a big drink of water. Cathy tells any patients who might be in the room to watch carefully. The second Penny has finished her water, she rushes to Cathy and puts her big, wet head in her lap and very coyly lifts her adoring brown eyes, as if to say, "I know you can't resist me." Looking down at her very wet slacks, Cathy laughs uproariously.

"Bringing joy and laughter is Penny's permanent job," Ms. Cathy says. It is routine.

Penny's workday begins.

"The most affectionate creature in the world is a wet dog."

— Ambrose Bierce

RESTORING MY SOUL

I was once asked how much I charged for Penny's visits. I had never even considered it. I heard myself say, "Nothing, there is no charge. I love doing it."

Then later, I started thinking about it. I am absolutely passionate doing what I do. The patients and the staff show their gratefulness in their faces. It appears that the line between giving and receiving has become quite fuzzy.

This compassion is what and who I am as a person. It is my passion.

This is my gift back to the world.

It restores my soul.

First Steps

Sometimes things just happen when you least expect them. Sometimes you try and try to do something, to force a result. Then I guess, not so surprisingly, when you let go and let a higher power take over, it does actually happen. Such was the case with Jim.

Penny had been visiting him for many, many months. Jim was paralyzed from the neck down. Each week both he and Penny looked forward to the sweetness of her golden head in his lap. And each time she was greeted with enthusiasm, optimism, and a big smile. I would take his hand and wrap my fingers around the top of his hand. By placing both of our hands on Penny's head, and moving them back and forth, he was able to feel her softness and let her know that she was appreciated and loved for her visits.

Each time he guaranteed us that "one day" he would be able to scratch her head by himself.

After getting permission and a release to photograph Jim, I sat Penny by his side and told her to "stay." As his therapist was busily adjusting braces on his legs, it was obvious Jim was totally absorbed in Penny, getting their picture taken together, and the moment. I backed up to focus the camera. When I looked through the lens, I noticed his hand was on top of Penny's head. I questioned this in my mind and assumed the therapist had placed it there, so I said nothing. Then totally astonished, the therapist asked Jim if he had moved his arm from his lap and placed his hand on Penny's head. He responded with resolute calmness, "I guess I did."

My beautiful golden girl was completely unaware of the wonder of it all. She only knew that the hand of a friend was on her head.

Life was good.

First steps!

THE SURVIVORS

Penny seemed to sense the excitement as we entered the rehabilitation gym. The "Welcome Waggin" had arrived. She had missed the past two weeks, due to a surgical procedure and her subsequent recovery, and she was "ready."

You see Penny herself is a cancer survivor. The staff knew first hand what she had faced and was facing, but the only thing on Penny's mind was saying "hi" to each and every one of her friends.

The patients (about sixty in number) were also beaming as we entered the room to extended hands and always the non-verbal expressions of smiles, points, eye contact, head nods, and gestures.

All of these were truly small miracles from courageous survivors.

As I glanced around the room, I noticed that Michael, a very special twenty year old we had been visiting weekly, was for the very first time following Penny with his eyes. Prior to this he simply stared silently into space. But this ordinary day, this glorious ordinary day, Penny walked up to his wheelchair and nudged his arm with her head. And almost effortlessly, he raised his arm and reached to pet her. I was carrying her brush, and without saying a word I handed it to him. He took it in his hand and softly brushed Penny's head and neck. As he did so, I knew that nothing would ever be the same.

With his therapist at my side, I sat silently as Michael and Penny shared something very special. I wondered if they knew what survivors they both were. I hugged Michael and told him that Penny had others to visit, and we would see him the next week and how very excited we were about his improvement.

He looked into her shining eyes and said, "Bye, Bye Penny." He had not spoken since being in the hospital.

"It's not what they give you; it's what they bring out in you."

— Anonymous

In a Heartbeat

It has been suggested that each year in a dog's life is equivalent to seven human years. Think about it. Perhaps this is because as we rush through each day, seemingly accomplishing very little, our furry friends are busy living seven times faster.

Watching Penny has taught me so much. I am convinced that the single most important lesson has been that of unconditional love.

She has seen me through personal tragedies where I didn't know if I could make it through the day. But looking deeply into her warm brown eyes, somehow I knew I had to.

It hasn't only been my life that she has impacted.

I watched as Jack's eyes brightened noticeably as he saw Penny in the rehab hospital. He held out his hand from his wheelchair, and Penny went right toward him.

His speech therapist who had been working with him realized Penny was going to take over for him for a little while. After having worked with and observed Penny and her patients, I have come to be intuitively aware of whether or not the patient wants to visit with both of us or spend private time with my little angel. It was quite clear that Jack wanted to visit only with Penny.

I backed up the length of the leash and began talking softly with the therapist, but always acutely aware of Penny and her needs, as well as the patient's. Jack began talking to Penny and telling her that he had dogs at home, but he wasn't able to remember their names. Penny didn't care if he knew their names or not. No judgment here! She was content to lay her head in his lap and continue their intimate conversation.

The speech therapist looked at me almost in total disbelief. He pulled me aside and whispered that Jack had spoken very little since his stroke, and this was the most he had spoken in weeks. It was wonderful to hear, but he continued to tell me that this was also the first time that Jack had actually formed entire sentences.

I just shook my head up and down, smiled, and realized that once again there was something wonderful working through my beautiful girl.

In just a heartbeat, a gigantic step had been taken and a lifetime begun.

FULL OF WONDER

When we entered the rehab gym, Francis was struggling, with the help of her therapist, to bend forward from a seated position. I watched, seeing how hard she was trying, but her efforts were futile and painful.

Penny sensed something. Out of the fifty patients in the room, she walked directly toward Francis. This wasn't all that unusual. On many visits, I simply let Penny choose the person she wants to visit.

This morning, as only a golden retriever can do, with quiet and serene confidence, Penny laid her head gently in the lady's lap.

Before you knew it, Francis was brushing her soft fur and seemingly, with great ease, she leaned completely forward to brush her very special new friend.

Penny's work was done. She had given Francis a very special gift and then simply melted at her feet and fell sound asleep. Francis smiled and then laughed out loud as she once again bent completely forward to see Penny's head resting on her foot.

All those observing were full of wonder, respect, and just a bit of reverence for what happened.

But no one was aware or prepared for what was about to happen.

Francis, quite suddenly realizing what she had achieved, smiled brightly and then summed it all up in one sentence. "There is no love as great as that of a dog."

Francis had not spoken in weeks.

"The best and most beautiful things in the world cannot be seen or even touched. They must be felt within the heart."

— Helen Keller

LISTENING WITH YOUR HEART

There are times when you don't have to do anything for something very important to happen.

As Penny enters the gym at the rehab hospital, she has no pressure, no judgments, no worries. She has only now. This is when you know that what needs to happen will happen. I have learned to just leave it alone. This is a very powerful message.

It is so awesome to just simply be there, watching wonderful things take place. Sometimes big things happen instantly, and then sometimes things happen that I won't learn about for several weeks, or even months, or perhaps ever.

Robert's was always the first outstretched hand we saw as we entered the gym. He was paralyzed and struggling each and every moment of the day. But in his face and in his eyes, I saw remarkable courage and determination. And each time he saw Penny, a bright, sincere, and contagious smile would appear. It seemed he truly loved her visits.

It was routine. I would take his hand in mine and hold it as I helped him pet her. He always told me he would one day be able to do it all by himself. I had no doubt about it.

After visiting with him for many months, one of his therapists told me that he was always so depressed and withdrawn until Fridays when Penny visited. I didn't understand. Could this be the only time he was animated and alive? The only time he showed joy? I was astonished.

There was something quite special between Robert and Penny.

The silent words spoken between them was truly something incredible to witness. Robert had the ears to hear, but he was listening with his heart.

It's not so much what Penny gave him, but what it brought out in him.

Robert is now home with his dogs and horses.

Listening!

HEARING THE SILENCE

There are a few emotions for which adequate words sometimes don't exist. I find myself facing piles of words to convey a feeling a patient might have, or that even I have as a witness to Penny's miracles.

Sometimes words aren't necessary. Sometimes words just get in the way. Sometimes it is nice to simply hear the silence and observe the softening eyes of a patient and the warm gentle eyes of my Penny.

"Take a good look into the eyes of your dog. If you don't see what I see, then spell dog backwards."
— Dr. Frank Vigue

THE SECRET

The stories of a lifetime can be told in a moment.

Penny had received a special invitation from the daughter of an elderly patient to visit her mother the next time we were in the hospital. Walking down the hallway to a patient who has requested a special visit with Penny, I find the feelings are always so intense.

When we entered the room, Beth's husband of sixty plus years was sitting on one bed and his wife on the other. She was noticeably quite frail. You could tell that the moment she saw Penny all of her previously loved and adored four-footed friends came flooding to her mind and to her heart.

Penny gently laid her head on Beth's lap. Within seconds both of her hands were enclosed over Penny's sweet face. She stroked her so gently and sensuously, it appeared to be a very spiritual experience.

Susan, the recreation therapist who was with us, quietly told Beth, "God so loved dogs that He gave them His name—only spelled backwards." Penny's new friend smiled faintly. She knew.

Sitting on the bed next to her, I gently scratched Beth's bare back with my fingertips. She sighed and whispered and said how good that felt as she continued to scratch Penny.

This was a valuable secret, quietly told. Each of us on this earth must love and care for the other. In sharing Penny's gifts, each of us in that room that day, that moment, experienced joy. I became suddenly aware that none of us should ever diminish the enormity of our lives and that precious place where love is.

This moment was a magical one where all things are possible.

"One word frees us of all the weight and pain of life: That word is love."

— Sophocles

ANGELA

Following a car accident and three weeks in the hospital for a brain injury, sixteen-year-old Angela was brought to rehab. Having no deficit awareness, she was impulsive, made poor decisions and had a short attention span.

But when Penny visited, she literally had a smile from ear to ear.

Normally quite negative, Angela became more positive when Penny was around. "I love this dog. Penny is great. Can she be my dog, too?"

Angela tended to think only of herself. The staff found that with Penny present Angela thought of others, was kinder, and her tone of voice changed. She told how Penny reminded her of her "old dog" and many good memories.

Penny gave her moral support and helped her get through the days, because she was excited about seeing "her" dog. Between visits, she had her photograph of Penny that was kept close at hand.

Angela seems to have said it best. "Penny is loveable to everyone. It doesn't matter who you are. Some people are conditional in their love, but Penny's love is unconditional. People respond to her when they won't respond to others. Penny is heaven sent. God put her here for a reason."

"Dogs are the most amazing creatures; they give unconditional love. For me they are the role model for being alive."

— Gilda Radner

THE TOOL BOX

For just a little over a year a very special, precocious two-year-old imperial shitzu, Sophie, had been working as Penny's partner at the rehab hospital. Seventy-eight-pound Penny and six-pound Sophie drew quite a crowd simply walking down the long halls at the hospital. They were an amazing team. Sophie, mesmerizing everyone she met, was truly a confident and adorable showstopper.

On this ordinary, and about to turn extraordinary day, we had just about completed our rounds in the rehab gym and were getting ready to leave when our attention was diverted to Joe in his wheelchair. As he glanced at the dogs, we couldn't help but notice that he was a robust, heavily-tattooed, strong, muscular, and seemingly isolated man who would be giving away his true self if he showed the slightest bit of interest in these comforting, unique therapists.

But something told me he needed them. As we approached him, the dynamics in the room dramatically changed. Joe softened. His eyes never left Sophie. Sophie's "mom," Judi, astutely asked if he would like to hold Sophie. He simply nodded okay. Little Sophie happily stood wagging on his lap, balanced on her tiny little back legs, gently licking his face and "giving kisses."

What happened next was a true awakening. Quite suddenly, Joe's deep hunger for a release came in an instant. His face contorted.

His eyes filled with tears, and he began sobbing uncontrollably.

He tried hard to apologize. He was a man and men don't cry. But he soon reached a point where he couldn't apologize, for his tears were honest and necessary. They were releasing the pain he had stored and ignored for so long since his accident.

I asked the nurse if he was okay. She simply shook her head that he was.

Judi, Penny, and I backed away, allowing Joe this unique medicine that he so desperately needed and this time alone, silently and unashamedly crying into this tiny six-pound furry miracle worker.

None of us wanted to remove Sophie from his lap, but it had been a long day and little Sophie was emotionally tired. She needed a rest, as did Joe. I mentioned to Judi that perhaps Joe would like a photograph of Sophie for his room. Judi handed him one and, through the tears, Joe revealed the true depth of his feelings for Sophie. He told Sophie that when he went back to work, he was going to put her picture on the inside lid of his toolbox where he could see her all the time.

Sometimes we need strength and support to get to the truth. Sometimes this comes in a very different package.

Joe would be okay!

"There is no psychiatrist in the world like a puppy licking your face."
— Ben Williams

THE CHRISTMAS GIFT

Penny had been visiting the Critical Care Unit of Methodist Hospital by special request from a very exhausted staff.

It was obvious the staff greatly enjoyed her visits, and she did seem to break, at least for a brief moment, the gravity of the life and death situations that continually hung in the balance.

Annie was a critical care patient, a very special patient. This 17- year-old girl had been in a very serious car accident and was not expected to live. Her family was at her bedside. Penny and I silently bypassed her room. The young girl's father came out, saw us, and without a word stopped and petted Penny on the head. I simply smiled.

The next week we returned expecting the young girl to not be there, but to our incredible amazement and delight she was sitting up and watching Penny visiting with the staff from her door. I knew we were supposed to be visiting the staff only, but I could see these pleading dark brown eyes watching Penny's every movement. After consulting with the head nurse, Penny and I were allowed to visit with Annie. She adored Penny and wanted so badly to pet her. But Annie was paralyzed from the neck down.

The following week, I had a telephone call from the chief nurse that Annie had been moved to a local rehab hospital, and Penny and I had been requested by Annie's therapist to visit her there.

The nurse had mentioned to the therapist how much Penny's visit had meant to Annie and felt it would be certainly worthwhile to continue these visits. This was all I needed to hear.

Each week for seven months, we visited with Annie. I would hold her hand and brush Penny, and we would laugh at how Penny "melted" to the floor when she saw the hairbrush. Each visit we could tell there had been just a little improvement. But Christmas Eve was special.

Annie had an extraordinary gift for Penny. We arrived, knocked on the door and asked Annie's mom if we could come in. She had a sheepish smile on her face, and as we walked in I soon understood why. Annie was sitting in a wheelchair (something she hadn't been able to do for months). What a wonderful Christmas gift.

Her mother explained that Annie had wanted so badly to thank Penny for all the visits and the confidence and love she gave her.

She was determined that the next visit, on Christmas Eve, for Penny she would be sitting in her wheelchair.

She also gave me a gift she was completely unaware of. I now am incredibly grateful for each and every movement I can make. As I sit at my computer, I bless Annie and her spirit, tenacity, and Christmas gift.

Today, in what you might perceive as a stressful moment, think of Annie and her struggle to move a hand, an arm, and to sit upright.

Remember her Christmas gift to Penny.

"Christmas is doing a little something extra for someone."

— Charles Schultz

THE LESSON

Our scars tell others of our will to live. And sometimes these scars teach others how to live. Such was the case one early morning at the rehab hospital.

With Penny close by my side, I was visiting with a strikingly beautiful, courageous middle-aged woman who was recovering from both of her legs being amputated just above the knee. It had been a drunk driver.

As she lay stroking Penny, she told me, "when you are going through these things, you simply find a way to deal with them."

What incredible words these were. I would have thought she would have been ashamed of her imperfection and angry. But I found, in this place of intentional healing, that it was quite the opposite.

You see she was making peace with her life. In Penny's calming presence, this lady, who I have never seen since that day, taught me an incredible lesson.

I am a different person from having spent just a few precious moments with her. Things, little things, stupid things, are a lot easier to deal with now.

I will never be the same again.

I wish I could thank her.

LAUGHTER IS THE BEST MEDICINE

The visit with Penny this particular week to many might have appeared uneventful. On the surface, there were no major breakthroughs and no obvious, remarkable, healing moments. But that was on the surface.

Penny's tail was wagging from the moment we got out of the car, walked down the hall, and entered the gym. As always, all heads turned. New patients did double takes when they saw Penny.

Some ignored her, at least for the moment. And then there is inevitably the audible chorus of "Hi Penny" from her old friends, staff and patients alike, all eager for their morning "hugs."

Penny "made the rounds," spreading her own kind of special medicine. One lady told Penny she was the "best medicine here. What you bring to people is something money can't buy. You should just see the look on people's faces when you come in."

And believe me, I will never tire of seeing those faces. It appears that pain eases and the struggles seem less difficult. And perhaps it is wishful thinking, but I do believe that Penny clears the room of negative energy as the burdens of the day begin.

My belief was proven when Penny was given the command to jump up on one of the mats with a patient most eager to "snuggle" her. Instantly, she backed up to the patient, turned over onto her back, and wiggled and stretched. Everyone was laughing at her antics. Within seconds, there were no less than five sets of hands on her, scratching her tummy and petting her golden head.

The laughter became contagious, as patients throughout the gym turned to see what was going on. Many joined in the laughing, and Penny obviously was thoroughly enjoying it. To her, she was getting her tummy scratched, and people were happy. What could be better?

Penny's special doggie medicine was easy to swallow. For those few moments, laughter really was the best medicine. It wasn't an uneventful day after all.

"The great pleasure of a dog is that you may make a fool of yourself with him and not only will he not scold you, but he will make a fool of himself too."
— Samuel Butler

THE WAITING ROOM

Penny and I had just completed our weekly visit to the Critical Care Unit at the hospital. The staff was always so gracious and thankful for Penny's brief time with them. And this time was certainly no exception.

Our visit was complete, and we headed out the door to the elevator directly across from the family's waiting area. There were four people sitting there, one man and three women. Three were quietly reading magazines. The third woman was on her cell phone silently crying. "Daddy just died."

I pressed the elevator call button, but Penny had something else in mind. Bypassing the other three people, she quite intentionally turned and walked directly to the young woman on the phone and put her head quietly in her lap. Without any hesitation or realization of what she was doing, the woman started stroking Penny's head as she continued her sad message on the phone.

This pose was held for about three or four minutes. For the two of them there was nothing else and nowhere else.

As the phone call ended, the woman very deliberately buried her face in Penny's neck and unashamedly sobbed.

Something very important was happening.

Penny offers a safe place to be, a place where people can be themselves. There are times I feel as if I am intruding.

"Awe is the finest portion of mankind...in awe one feels profoundly the immense."

— Goethe

THE LINT ROLLER

As Penny and I "make the rounds" at the hospital, I always carry a red and tan L.L. Bean™ canvas bag embroidered with a golden retriever and the word "Penny." In this bag, you will find a hair brush, a bag of treats, a water bowl, a photo album with pictures of Penny's friends, antibacterial wipes, tissues, squeeze toys, a "Kong" ball and other toys that help the patients with dexterity, and what I thought was important, a lint roller.

As much as I bathe and groom Penny prior to visiting, she still sheds her golden hair. I always offer the lint roller to patients and staff alike.

Usually the use of the lint roller is declined. I continually found this odd. Finally I asked one lovely lady who had spent fifteen minutes telling Penny all about her pets at home, how terribly she missed them, and how they missed her, too, if she would like the lint roller.

She answered quite simply, "I feel like I am at home with dog hair on my slacks."

Penny quite unknowingly found the opportunity to give the gift of home, if only for a moment.

Her souvenir.

> *"I talk to him when I'm lonesome like; and I'm sure he understands. When he looks at me so attentively, and gently licks my hands; then he rubs his nose on my tailored clothes, but I never say naught thereat. For the good Lord knows I can buy more clothes, but never a friend like that."*

— W. Dayton Wedgefarth
From his poem "Bum"

An Awakening

This particular day, I woke up feeling peaceful and full of energy and enthusiasm about another visit with Penny at the rehab hospital. But I didn't know that what would happen this day would be life changing for me.

As we walked into a gym full of much activity, we were immediately called to a particular patient. Penny and I had visited briefly with this lady a week or two before, but my recollection of that visit was dim. On any specific day, we can visit with 35 to 60 patients.

Anne was sitting at a table with her therapist. She called me to her and asked if I knew why Penny was ignoring her. I told her I wasn't aware that she was. Inside I was concerned that this lady was feeling rejected by Penny in some manner.

She proceeded to tell me that she had lung cancer. "You see I have the will to live. I really do. Penny knows that and she also knows that I have no power to spare for her. You see she ignores me, because she knows. The first time she came to me, she took my power. After she left, I was exhausted. I had nothing left for myself."

Not being absolutely certain what she was telling me, I shared with Anne that Penny was a cancer survivor. She seemed somehow to know this, as she told me that Penny "was surviving on the love of others. You see we are both survivors. We are invincible, and we have God's love."

Anne then said she had something else to tell me that was important that I should remember. Gently, quietly, and looking deeply past my eyes and into my soul she said, "When you are depleted of all energy and when Penny is depleted as well, and you have nothing else to give, simply turn yourselves over to God. He will hold you up. He will support you until you are rested. Never forget to take care of yourselves." This was what she was trying to tell me. It was time for her to take care of herself. She had no energy to spare.

She also understood, in that large room full of struggling, exhausted, and sometimes depleted individuals, that Penny and I very often leave for home exhausted with nothing else to give. This unexpected message, from an unexpected source, granted me something I had needed for a long time— permission to care for myself.

We visited other patients that morning, but soon Penny and I needed to go home. I had always been taught to give, to work till I couldn't anymore, to feed the world, but never myself. I now understood.

This extraordinary lesson was learned. To be able to survive on the love of others, we must first love ourselves.

My old identity was shattered.

My new one was emerging.

> "Just when the caterpillar thought the world was over, it became a butterfly."
>
> — Anonymous

THE MARINE

He was young. He was brave, and he had been severely wounded.

John had been protecting his country in Iraq.

He told me his story as he waited for his next painful therapy session. While we talked, he never once stopped petting Penny.

His fingers gently massaged the top of her head, her ears and her neck. If he slowed, Penny would remind him by silently nudging his arm. He would smile.

John never complained or grimaced, but I knew he was hurting. His recovery would take at least another year or longer. I felt so proud to know him and honored that he chose to share his story with me.

A week later, our second meeting was in his room. John was packed and waiting on his military escort to go back to Walter Reed Hospital in Washington D.C.

Penny and I sat and waited with him. This was the only gift we had for him. A thank you of sorts. He told me how much her presence meant to him. And then he said, "When I die, God will have to retire all of my angels. They have been very busy protecting me, and they must be very tired. You see, Penny has been but one."

As the escort approached down the long hall, John said I reminded him of his mom and asked if he could hug me. As he hugged me, at that precise moment, he was my son and his mom was in the room.

"Dogs are our link to paradise. They don't know evil or jealousy or discontent. To sit with a dog on a hillside on a glorious afternoon is to be back in Eden, where doing nothing was not boring—it was peace."
— Milan Kundera

CAROLE

I can say in all honesty that I have never been in another health care facility or any workplace where the entire staff is smiling, caring, sensitive, professional, dedicated, and obviously happy and enthusiastic to be doing what they are doing. I hear over and over again from patients who are going home that they unquestionably owe their recovery to the therapists and the hospital. What an incredible statement.

The RIOSA staff truly thrives on Penny's visit. We walk into the gym or down the hall and it is "Hi Penny!" For a year I don't think anyone knew my name. I was quite simply "Penny's mom."

Carole has always been a favorite of Penny's and visa versa. When asked how her patients benefit from Penny's visits, she puts it quite succinctly. "Unconditional love is a wonderful feeling that so few receive and so few know how to give. The twinkle in patients' eyes lights up a room when they see Penny heading their way.

"Her love and attention seem to put all the patients on an even scale. Everyone seems to feel 'okay' when Penny is around. All of the sadness, hopelessness, or helplessness disappears as the patients run their fingers through her beautiful, soft, flowing fur.

"The focus seems to switch from thoughts of loneliness or sadness to giggles and funny stories about their own pets."

Carole admits that she has had some struggles with loneliness and depression. "I have always been able to count on my lab, Beau, for the unconditional love that I don't know if I've ever received or given. Penny makes me feel that same way."

Carole has moved on, but a picture of Penny is in her apartment.

"I know that she truly is a gift, an amazing gift that brings me a special joy that is hard to describe."

Carole has a new man in her life, and she looks forward to introducing him to Penny "so he can fall in love with her, too."

Penny, a blessing during hardships, shows once again that love is indeed a healing thing.

"Some friends leave footprints in your heart."
— Eleanor Roosevelt

THE BUSINESS OF NOW

Far too many of us seem to worry about what didn't get done yesterday and what all we have to accomplish tomorrow. What if quite suddenly we didn't know if we would have a tomorrow?

Valerie, a 32-year-old mother of three and a social worker, was diagnosed with a spinal tumor. Surgery was critical. No promises were given. She spent all of her time prior to surgery making plans, talking to her parents, loving her children, preparing. She told the doctors if there was no hope to "close her up."

She found flowers to smell, her baby's neck to cuddle, and clouds to watch. She was afraid. Afraid she wouldn't see her children grow up and that she would be cheated of the rest of her life.

Surgery proved the tumor benign, but the doctors told her because of the location, she would most likely not walk again. She disagreed. "I have three boys to raise. I will walk."

When Penny and I met her, she was smiling as she told us her story.

"Twenty-four hours after surgery, I was walking. I showed them!" She beamed. There were other plans for her. Valerie told me she would never again take anything for granted.

The simplest little thing was a miracle for her.

Penny and I took a break to go outside for a few minutes. I picked a very tiny flower (the blossom only one-eighth of an inch across) from the grass. Penny and I took it back in to Valerie. As I handed it to her, I knew she understood. We both did.

As Valerie petted Penny, she quite casually announced that she is going to law school to become a disabilities attorney. I don't doubt it for a moment.

"Life is not about being right or wrong. It's not about having the correct information, or the proper answers. It's not about playing the right notes. Life is about hearing the music. In other words, it's not the number of breaths you take that gives you life; it is the number of moments that take your breath away. Most people go through life asleep. But the ones who are awake live in constant total amazement. We can practice the sacrament of the blessed present, knowing each moment can be infused with the sacred."

— Terry Hershey, Hallmark Channel, Author
Sacred Necessity: Gifts for Living with Passion,
Purpose and Grace (Sorin Books)
Soul Gardening: Cultivating the Good Life
(Augsburg Fortress)
Storyteller, philosopher, humorist, motivational speaker

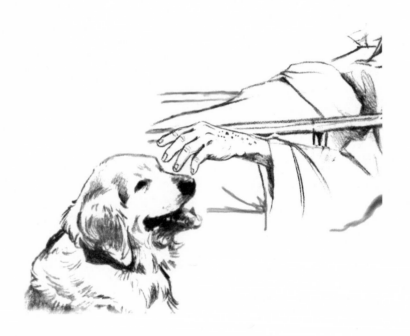

ONE TOUCH

Penny and I had entered the hospital when we were immediately intercepted. A nurse told us that she had a patient who had cried out all night for her dog and had not slept at all.

We went directly to her room. Elaine, battling cancer, was lying in bed staring at the ceiling. I walked up to her and told her I understood she had been asking for her dog, and that I had a special visitor for her.

Penny approached her and laid her head on the edge of the bed.

Elaine was very weak, so I asked if I could put her hand on Penny's head. She simply nodded that it was okay.

Her fingers moved quietly and calmly as she caressed Penny, but I knew in her heart and mind she was petting her own dog.

Within a matter of moments, Elaine fell into a peaceful, restful sleep, with her hand still on Penny's head.

Sometimes things just can't be questioned.

"My little old dog: A heartbeat at my feet."
— Edith Wharton

SPECIAL IN THE ORDINARY

It wouldn't have appeared to be anything special to most people. But to Angie and Ed a mountain was moved.

Penny and I had been working with Ed to use his left arm as he recovered from a brain aneurysm and a very long hospitalization.

He could move the fingers on his left hand and was able to hold a small piece of a dog biscuit. The therapist, supporting him at the elbow, asked Ed to move his arm slowly to hand Penny the treat. I gave Penny the command to "leave it." To her, it must have seemed like hours, but she never once tried to take the biscuit.

Fred moved a fraction of an inch at a time. But he was moving. As Ed's fingers, holding the treat, reached her nose, I said "okay!"

After exhibiting incredible patience, this hard-won treat was consumed in a second.

The therapist, Angie, and I all cheered. Fred smiled from ear to ear. We repeated this process four or five times.

Ed was getting weary so I gave him a hug and told him Penny and I would see him next week.

As we turned to go, something told me to turn and look back.

As I did so, I saw Angie look at her husband with such incredible love. She leaned over to him, he slowly raised his head, and they kissed each other with such great love and gentleness. I quickly turned away. I felt as if I had intruded upon a very private moment.

I had just seen a glimpse into heaven.

"The journey of a thousand miles must begin with a single step." — Chinese Proverb

The Randomness of Life

Ernie, a paranoid schizophrenic, was homeless and had been for a long time. He went to sleep one evening, and the next morning he woke up in the hospital.

A drunk driver had hit him.

Kelly, an attorney, had volunteered her services to try to find out his name and if he had any relatives. She became his guardian.

I met Kelly in the rehab hospital. She asked if Penny and I had time to visit with Ernie. We went to his room and, without a moment's hesitation, Penny walked directly to him, her tail wagging, and laid her precious head on his knees. She offered him something he had rarely been offered, love and affection. He placed both of his weathered, rough hands on her head and began stroking her fur. The feel of something so soft was foreign to him. This unconditional and non-judgmental four-footed therapist was just what the doctor ordered. He began quietly whispering to her. Words I couldn't hear. It didn't matter.

He took her head and pulled her close to his chest and gently kissed her. In a few moments, I asked if he would like for Penny to visit him next week. "Well sure, why not!"

His attorney picked up his dirty clothes, put them in a bag, and we left Ernie's room. Walking down the hallway Kelly said, "If they are over fifty and homeless, no one gives a damn. I will find him something to do when he gets out of here. I will."

She turned toward the parking lot, taking his laundry home with her.

"Sometimes in observing one small gesture, you can know someone completely."

— Greeting card

THE BEACH

It was late September. I was at the beach, tuning out and turning inward. The silence of the place in off-season was just what I needed. It had been a very long and extremely painful year for me, full of introspection and healing. Time had been both my enemy and my friend.

As I sat, peacefully absorbed in watching the waves roll in and out, the quiet was interrupted when the phone rang. It was Rosie, a patient at the rehab hospital. She had called to tell me the date was set for her surgery the following day to remove her cancerous lung.

She loved Penny, and Penny loved her so much. She wanted "us" to know.

It may seem odd, but I wanted to tell Penny. I needed to share my fears for Rosie with her. But she was two hundred miles away. "No dogs allowed" at the condo. Penny would have cared. Through instinct or intuition, she would have understood.

I had met Rosie only a handful of weeks ago. My resolve to not get personally involved with "our" patients dissolved when I met this remarkable woman.

I rather quickly learned that Rosie was not to be defined by her illness, but rather by her spirit, her faith, and her remarkable courage.

She knew Penny was also a cancer survivor. They shared something quite extraordinary.

To Rosie, courage is like breathing. Twenty-eight years ago her husband of nineteen "precious" years passed away. She told me that he had come out of a three-day coma for just a few moments to hold her hand and tell her it would be okay. "He is still the love of my life." She never remarried.

I will forever hold in my heart our last visit with the three of us in a room full of sixty-plus people. She quietly held one arm and open hand toward heaven and the other hand she placed on Penny's head.

She told me that the power of God was flowing from her uplifted hand, through her body, into Penny, and back again. Their strength would be replenished. Something very personal and powerful had just happened.

After I hung up the phone, I realized that watching the waves roll onto the shore and then back out to sea, replenishes my soul in much the same way.

I missed Penny. I'm quite sure she is able to feel a human's pain in her heart.

The Hurricane

I was sitting in a beachfront condo at a glass top round table, looking out the window at the waves gently caressing the shore, watching seagulls, sandpipers, pelicans, and a solitary fisherman standing in the surf.

The television tells me that Hurricane Rita is heading this way and evacuation is imminent. It will hit the Texas Gulf Coast in three days. The sky is a brilliant blue and there is a black bird perched on the back of a green plastic lawn chair on the fourth floor balcony.

Tomorrow I leave the island. The car is full of gas and bags are beginning to be packed. There is a gnawing feeling of apprehension and the possible devastation yet to come. Will the condo be here in a week?

I think of Penny waiting at home 160 miles away. I have learned from her the possibilities of living for the moment.

Relax and breathe. Breathe out the fear. Sometimes we don't have to look ahead. All we have is now. It is the right place to be.

Funny that this lesson has taken me over half of my life to learn.

Soon Penny will be curled at my feet. Peace and comfort are waiting.

This is a lesson in just being. But for now, wherever I am is the right place to be.

I go do the laundry.

GOLDEN VALUES

I suppose my values are not much different than Penny's.

Love like there is no tomorrow.

Be happy no matter what someone does to you.

Lie in the grass on a warm summer day.

Stretch before getting up.

Beg for a long walk.

Be fascinated with a simple routine.

Enjoy eating the same food every day.

Do the responsible thing even though it isn't always popular.

Act goofy once in a while, just because.

Drink lots of water.

When you're happy, wag your whole body.

Be loyal.

Eat with great enthusiasm.

Rejoice at the wind in your face.

Play daily.

If someone is hurting, sit real close, be very quiet and softly nuzzle them.

Yes

As I work on this book of stories, Penny is napping at my feet.

She stretches, rolls over, but not before lazily looking up at me, to make certain I am still in my chair.

It comforts her.

It comforts me.

We're both where we are meant to be.

HAVING IT ALL

Perhaps it comes from having had to clean out my mother's and my mother-in-law's homes when they passed away. What does one do with a hundred pair of hose? Three unused crepe pans, jelly jars of baby teeth, locks of hair, and love letters from young restless boys of long ago.

Suddenly, I remember when I was a young girl having to sit at the kitchen sink polishing sterling silver that we never were allowed to use. Heaven forbid!

My mother would be horrified if she saw me using it every day in my own home.

Sure I have things I don't use. But I very willingly and happily purge myself of these unused things once or twice a year. I feel good when I simplify. The things remaining are more special, more loved and meaningful. These things purposely chosen to remain really matter; I hold them dear in my heart.

So many have to have more and more until their garages, closets, and cupboards are bursting. Material *minutia.*

But how do they feed their souls? How do they contribute to the significance of others' lives?

My Penny shines with examples of qualities we would all do well to imitate.

"Surely, there must be more to life than having everything."

— Maurice Sendak

Loss

An evacuee from New Orleans in the aftermath of Hurricane Katrina was sent to "our" rehab hospital in San Antonio.

He saw Penny and his eyes filled with tears. He was a large, strong looking man, seemingly able to handle anything.

With enormous sadness he said, "I lost my house. I lost my dog. I lost everything. I can live without my house, but my dog. I'm not sure."

I felt his pain.

This hurricane proved that people would rather risk anything than leave their beloved pets behind.

"One place understood, helps us understand all other places better."

— Eudora Welty

FOOTSTEPS

Sometimes I think I may call him too often. But then I know I don't. Penny's veterinarian is a godsend. He understands. He has held my hand and knows my heart. He has been with me during some of the darkest days of my life. He doesn't need to be told how important Penny is to me and to so many others.

I assume most of you are dog lovers and know the intense pain and almost unbearable loss when you have to release one of your beloved pets. We all know it is the right and loving thing to do.

But that doesn't make it any easier. A part of us goes with them.

And it is a blessing that a part of them stays with us forever.

My first therapy dog, and one of the first "legal" ones in San Antonio, was Casey. Casey had been a "generic" rescue from the dog pound at eight weeks of age. He had been locked in a car in over 110 degrees in San Antonio in August. A good Samaritan broke into the car in order to rescue him. He remained at the dog pound for a month. No one came forward to claim him. And for good reason. They would have been charged with animal cruelty.

I had been on television producing and hosting an Adopt a Pet segment on the 5:00 P.M. newscast for many years. It didn't take long before I was told of this "little dog at the pound with a very big heart and so much personality." But the law said that he had to be "put down" if his owners didn't claim him. That wasn't going to happen. There was something very special about him. Little did I know how true that was.

After much confusion, I got a court order to get him released into the custody of the humane society. They, in turn, turned him over to me literally within moments of what would have been his last breath.

I had Casey for twenty-one years. He was my best friend and a lifeline for many elderly residents in several long-term care facilities, as well as to many little children with cancer.

I knew the day would come, but twenty-one years is a very long time. Dr. Earl was right there with me. He was calm, reassuring, and most of all—understanding. I couldn't get the words out for an hour. But with his strong presence, a sense of peace, and my heart telling me that the only and last loving gift I could give my best friend, I was able to say good-bye and tell my Casey that I would see him again one day. His passing was painless. Only I felt the pain.

The last several months of his life, he chased me around the kitchen in his K-9 Cart. What fun he had. He never took his eyes off of me, no matter where I was. I would carry him from room to room because I knew he needed and wanted to be where he could see me. It has been three years this August since I lost Casey. But there isn't a day that passes that I don't think of him and his devotion, patience, and the joy he brought to so many, in much the same way as Penny.

How I loved that dog. His legacy truly lives on.

"I know you're shining down on me from Heaven, like so many friends we've lost along the way. And I know eventually we'll be together, one sweet day."

—Mariah Carey and Boyz 2 Men
"One Sweet Day"

TAKING THE LEAD

Beth was on her knees when we walked into the rehab gym. Her elbows were resting on an elevated mat and her knees on a lower mat. Her therapist by her side, she was learning how to get up should she ever fall. She was using her elbows to walk across the mat and then pull the rest of her up. She had no use of her legs.

The concentration, pain, and frustration were so very evident in her face. She tried and tried to no avail. Tears came.

Observing closely, I couldn't decide if we should approach or not. But not so surprising, Miss Penny made that decision for me.

You would think, after all the remarkable things I have witnessed with Penny, that I would never be caught off guard. But this time I truly was.

Penny took the lead and confidently walked over to the lady. She put her front paws on the elevated mat right next to Beth. And in all honesty, Penny started pulling herself up onto the mat, in much the way the therapist was trying to help Beth to do.

Beth's frustration and tears instantly turned to laughter. Everyone in the gym turned to watch this golden soul turned teacher. I had to follow the trail of hugs to find Penny.

Call it what you will, but for that moment, life couldn't get any better.

It was a day of hope and courage.

If I can stop one heart from breaking,
I shall not live in vain.
If I can ease one life the aching,
Or cool one pain,
Or help one fainting robin
Unto his nest again.
I shall not live in vain.

— Emily Dickinson

Through the Eyes of Others

One patient always seemed especially excited to spend time with Penny. And I must admit, quite often we managed to spend a few extra minutes with her.

Every week I noticed a bit more improvement than the week before as she struggled and fought to walk. You couldn't help but be aware of the courage and sheer determination in her face.

Sitting a short distance away and watching her every movement, her family members were almost always there to support her. This particular day they weren't there. I asked her where they were and she simply said "they hadn't come." I told her that made Penny happy, because she could have all of her attention.

She looked into Penny's warm soft brown eyes, took her face in her hands. With tears in her eyes, she told Penny how saddened she always was by her family members because of the pain that she saw in their eyes while they watched her struggling to walk again. They had unknowingly and unintentionally caused her more pain.

But this day, with Penny in attendance expecting nothing, asking nothing, and promising nothing, this charming lady was able to focus on what she had to do and not on the pain she was causing others.

This day, free from the pain in someone else's eyes, she walked a few wonderful, precious steps, joyfully laughing, with Penny by her side.

"Animals are such agreeable friends – they ask no questions, they pass no criticisms."

— George Eliot

MARGARET ROSE

It started out as an uneventful day, running multiple necessary errands. I was stopped at a red light and was drawn to a sign for a pediatric dental office. Without a single breath, a thought came to me, and I could not get rid of it. I had more stops to make, but before I knew it I was driving directly back to my office. I had never heard of pet-assisted therapy in a dental office working with fearful children. It would work. I had no doubt about it.

Within minutes I was in my office, phone book in my lap. The first ad I saw in pages and pages of ads clearly stood out from all the rest. "Parents allowed back with children." I immediately liked this dentist. If parents were allowed, why not Penny?

I picked up the phone and called the dental clinic. Before I knew it, Penny had a new part-time job.

Little fair-skinned, red-haired Margaret Rose was eight and very fearful of dentists because of a previous bad experience.

Full of anticipation, Penny and I arrived at the dental office at 8:30 A.M. Margaret Rose, her mom, "aunt by love," and the entire staff stood at the window to welcome the new furry dental assistant. It occurred to me that Margaret Rose and Penny had the same color hair.

Penny, ignoring the new surroundings, smells, and unknown people, went directly to her new little friend and lay down at her feet. Yes, it was meant to be.

I was also meant to see the sign (literally and figuratively) at that stop light. Penny and Margaret Rose were supposed to meet.

Penny stayed by her side while her pre-anesthesia took effect.

Penny's calming and comforting demeanor, I like to think, played a part in relaxing Margaret Rose as well. It wasn't such a big scary world, as long as Mom, aunt, and Penny were close by.

The dentist, loving and kind, gently stroked her patient's red hair.

Speaking calmly and reassuringly the entire time, she allowed Margaret Rose to be in control. "Do you want a drink, do you need to swallow, you are doing so great, Punkin. The hard part is over."

Words like bubblegum flavor, Mr. Tickler, a raincoat for your teeth, Mr. Whistler came from the dentist's mouth, as if a bedtime story was being told. *Pocahantas* played on a screen in the background.

Margaret Rose was a strong little girl. We stayed in the room with her the entire time. Once or twice this brave little patient moaned a tiny little moan. Penny's eyebrows raised and her ears perked up in concern for her new friend. But beneath the dental chair, the noises, and the strangeness, Penny was as good as gold, waiting patiently.

Soon Margaret Rose was eating her favorite, chocolate ice cream.

Penny had a treat, a walk, and Margaret Rose gave her some water and a big hug before leaving to go tell Dad all about it.

Life was good.

THE WEE LASSIE

Mrs. McIntosh was from Scotland. She exuded a wonderful sense of humor and quite a bit of spunk. When I first met her, she was sitting in the recreation room reading the morning paper when Penny came through the door, preparing to scatter love throughout the room.

She saw Penny and put down the newspaper. "Oh, look at the wee laddie. Isn't he handsome?"

I told her that she wasn't a "laddie," but rather a "lassie."

Penny went up to her and as always put her pretty head in the lap of this lady with the twinkling eyes.

Mrs. McIntosh started petting Penny and looking into the softest brown eyes anywhere.

"You know, lassie, it doesn't matter whether you are a lad or a lassie, does it?"

Obviously distracted and just a little irritated by our conversation, the lady in the next wheelchair put down the newspaper she had been reading and with great exasperation said, "Oh, good heavens! It doesn't matter – laddie or lassie. It's just all cosmetic anyway."

Everyone laughed.

At that exact moment I realized that it was better to be me than anyone else on earth.

LISTENING

The simple act of intentional listening as Penny and I walk the length of the gym through seeming crowds of people who are afraid, lonely, tired, grumpy, sad, struggling, or in pain is a lesson in itself.

"Oh, that hurts."

"Look at that dog."

"I don't know what to do next."

"I'm cold."

"Which is my therapist?

"I'm trying to find the swimming pool."

"I'll just sit here and wait. I'm trying."

"Aren't these the greatest people here?"

"I get to go home tomorrow to see my dog."

"Michael, look up. Good job."

"One more time. You're doing great."

"Oh, look. There's Penny. Penny here, here! Look at her eyes. Oh, she is so beautiful. Look at her eyelashes."

Sounds of healing.

BLESSINGS

As autumn arrives, there is a procession of animals led to churches for The Blessing of the Animals. This custom is conducted in remembrance of St. Francis of Assisi's love for all creatures. This bond between people and their pets is like no other relationship, because here you will find that communication is at its most basic.

This deep bond draws many, many people to church with their "best friends" by their side.

On a sunny Sunday afternoon, I, too, took the opportunity to take Penny to church for this special blessing. Penny waited patiently in a sanctuary full of no less than eighty or ninety dogs, cats, ferrets, and birds. At the altar, there was a beautiful shiny brass cross and two white stuffed fluffy puppy dogs. The welcome was beautiful.

> "We are gathered here today because we have all experienced a miracle in our lives, the miracle of having a friend who is an animal. Each of you came today not just to have our animals blessed but to have your friendship with them blessed. We all know the wondrous experience of looking into the eyes of an animal friend and recognizing that we understand each other perfectly, that heart is speaking to heart, without need for words."

Penny was the last to receive the blessing. We approached the altar, and I told Reverend Donna Strieb how very grateful we were for her doing this. I told her of Penny's special ministry at the rehabilitation hospital and of the patients and staff who loved her so much and also of her battle with cancer. She knelt down beside Penny and placed her hand lightly on Penny's head. Penny looked so peaceful and beautiful.

The prayer for her was different than for the others. Reverend Strieb asked for a special blessing for this angel of mercy that she could continue her extraordinary work and healing love with people in need and that her cancer would remain in remission. And that she and I would enjoy our life together and find joy with the God who created us both. Her final prayer in this sacred place was so meaningful.

"O Lord, give us humility to thank You for the creation of animals, who can show affection which sometimes puts us to shame. Enlarge our respect for these your creatures, of whom we are the guardians. And give us a sense of responsibility towards them, for Jesus Christ's sake. Amen."

Penny was given a beautiful blue ribbon to tell the world she was truly blessed. We went to the church courtyard for special bone-shaped doggie treats and then home with a full heart.

Those warm brown adoring eyes of my little angel in disguise seemed especially bright that night as I rubbed my face into her warm wonderful dog fur.

Aware

I had been visiting my daughter and her husband in Montana and took a side trip to Jackson Hole, Wyoming. As a lover of art, the galleries were irresistible. It wasn't until months later that I would know how irresistible.

The first one I passed had a welcoming open door. I glanced inside and instantly was mesmerized by an oil painting of a wolf. I walked in and knew that that painting had to be mine. I had never felt this way before about a work of art.

I stood in front of it for several moments, transfixed. "Aware" was a profile of the most beautiful animal I had ever seen. The focus, determination, courage, and strength of this wolf were enormously powerful. I could not explain why I was so drawn to this particular painting.

With a lump in my throat, I literally felt the painting affording me the attributes of this magnificent animal.

I put a deposit on the painting. When I got home, I felt strangely renewed and courageous enough to begin writing this book. This is something I had always wanted to do, but never with enough confidence to actually write it.

I was looking forward to the day when the painting would arrive at my front door. But I found myself wondering if it would still hold the same feelings in me.

One early, early morning, I had an inexplicable dream that seemed strangely childlike and at the same time disturbing and haunting.

In this dream, a large wooden crate arrived with several screws holding it together. It was "the" painting. I carefully unscrewed the crate, and as each screw was removed, I became more and more excited.

As I opened the box, I found I wasn't able to see the wolf until I had removed twenty-five or more sheets of paper, one at a time, from the painting. On each of the twenty-five sheets, in different places, was a painting of Tinkerbell from *Peter Pan* sprinkling golden fairy dust on each page. I removed the pages one at a time and then finally the beautiful wolf appeared.

I woke up and could not go back to sleep, wondering what this strange dream meant.

I later was telling a friend about it. As I detailed the dream for her, the answer came to me quite clearly. As I removed each page, I was removing a page of my pain, my anger, my betrayal, my fear, my unhappiness, my past life, my inability to forgive. After all the pages of my past were removed, there was the beauty (in the guise of the wolf) and my future, a beautiful future that would surely be blessed with courage, determination, and strength.

As my future will be, the painting arrived and was received with a song of great joy and celebration of spirit.

According to Native American beliefs, the brown wolf is my spirit guide. Wolf will be there to assist me to achieve the harmony and discipline necessary to control and direct my own life and the power to recognize that I control my own reality with loyalty, honor, and integrity. The wolf will guard me and teach me with great love. And according to Native American beliefs, when wolf shows up, it is time to take control of one's life and redirect it to find the true spirit of freedom.

So with a single painting, this book began, as well as the first day of the rest of my life.

THE MISSED VISIT

Penny had to miss a visit to the hospital because of a medical problem. We ended up at the animal hospital instead.

I was feeling very unsettled that we were going to miss one of the patient's birthdays. It was a tremendous milestone because of her battle with cancer.

Penny and I sat in the waiting room until the veterinary technician came to take Penny to the back. I sat very quietly in the waiting room, concerned for "my girl" with her heart of gold.

I noticed a pretty woman with short hair, hoop earrings, and a smile that wouldn't stop, sitting with an apricot poodle on her lap.

It was obvious this pup meant the world to her and visa versa. She was looking at him with such deep love. I asked his name and she told me, "This is Jerry. He is my life!" She continued telling me that a year ago she was diagnosed with cancer and had to undergo chemotherapy. Her doctor suggested she get a pet.

Jerry entered her life as a little year old puppy, the runt in a litter no one wanted. "He never left my side. He knew when I was feeling so very sick, and he knew how much I needed him."

You see, when she was diagnosed with cancer, her husband left her. Jerry had become her life, her lifeline, and medicine she could hug. Jerry had brought her great peace and comfort in the midst of incredible pain. He had given life back to her.

On the way home, I called my friend and wished her a happy birthday and explained to her why we couldn't visit her that day. I cried as I told her of Jerry and his "mom."

"Although the world is full of suffering, it is also full of the overcoming of it." — Helen Keller

PAW PRINTS

I never cease being amazed at what Penny awakens in her patients.

Their relationship is an intensely intimate one. There is often a moment in time where I feel my presence is intrusive. These people tell Penny of their pain, despair, feelings of loss, and of their struggles to get better.

"I knew it would be a good day. Penny is so special. She was sent here to help me through today. I was scared until I saw her."

This special therapy dog often stands between hope and despair.

Penny, with great grace and gentleness in her soul, undoubtedly is leaving paw prints in the hearts of those struggling to heal.

Success stories are hard to argue with.

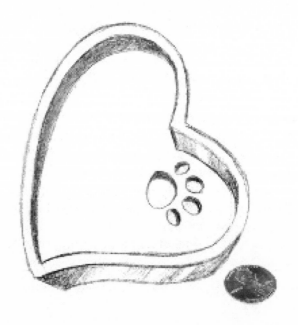

THE BIRTHDAY GIRL

February 20, 2004, Penny was given a very special eighth birthday party by the patients and staff at the hospital.

A large eight-foot table was colorfully decorated. There were two cakes, one chocolate and one German chocolate, punch, balloons, and baskets of homemade dog biscuits made by the patients especially for Penny and her furry friends.

The newspaper had been alerted and was sending a photographer.

Billy showed up just as the festivities were about to begin. He told me that he only had 15 or 20 minutes to spend with us. But I was so pleased he was there that 15 minutes sounded great.

I told him we had only certain patients who had signed release forms to be photographed. He kindly understood and honored that.

The patients didn't seem to care in the least that there was a photographer there. As usual, all eyes were on Penny. One gentleman was holding out his arm to her. We went to visit with him, and from the corner of my eye I saw Billy watching very closely from a distance. This busy photographer appeared to soften, and slowly it wasn't just his job to be there anymore. I recognized what had happened. Billy was hooked. He had become a part of the wonder of it all.

He took wonderful, sensitive photographs of Penny and her hospitalized friends and stayed with us to enjoy cake and punch.

Penny sat with her head in his lap, seemingly thanking him for coming. I glanced at my watch and was surprised to see that Billy had been with us two hours. I apologized for keeping him there for so long and gave him a big hug.

He said, "I am a better person for having been here today."

Billy understood!

Penny's Grrrreat Doggie Treats

The patients and staff had a great time making these for Penny's birthday party. Just remember, these are treats and should be given only for special occasions and with your veterinarian's blessings.

Yield 3-4 dozen.

2-1/2 cups whole wheat flour
1/2 cup powdered dry milk
1/2 t. salt
1/2 t. garlic powder
1 t. brown sugar
6 T. margarine or meat drippings
1 egg, beaten
1/2 cup ice water

Preheat oven to 350 degrees. Combine flour, dry milk, salt, garlic powder and brown sugar. Cut in margarine until mixture resembles cornmeal. Mix in egg and enough ice water so mixture forms a ball. Pat or roll out dough. Using a dog-bone shaped biscuit cookie cutter, cut out dog treats. Re-roll scraps and cut out.

Place on lightly oiled cookie sheet. Bake in preheated oven for 25-20 minutes. Remove from oven and cool on a wire rack.

PRECIOUS MOMENTS

It was gently raining outside. The skies were gray, and the grass appeared to be growing by the second. The phone was silent. It was peaceful—the perfect time to write.

It must have been two or three hours that I sat at the computer writing Penny's stories. All my dogs, Penny, Lulu, Wally, and Baby Grace, were asleep in different corners of my office. As I looked around at these little caretakers and bundles of love, I felt truly blessed.

I got up from my desk and decided to take a well-deserved break. I lay down on the floor for a few moments to do some yoga stretches. Within a second, Penny curled up under my arm. The others were quite busy getting my attention, licking, nuzzling, and tumbling over me. It was obvious that they were happy to have me on their level, and they were undoubtedly doing all they could to take advantage of it.

The yoga didn't work out, but the love did.

On this dreary rainy day, there was suddenly a ray of golden sunshine.

A day I learned to never misplace a precious moment.

"I think I could turn and live with animals, they're so placid and self-contained, I stand and look at them long and long."

— Walt Whitman (1819-1892)
"Song of Myself"

Time Off

Penny and I had not been able to visit the hospital for three weeks, due to a "hot spot" and an unexpected reaction to a medication.

Not visiting our patients bothered me. I knew they would be waiting and wondering. I missed them.

But I soon realized it wasn't about me. I knew Penny needed to heal, in much the same way as her patients.

I watched her, cared for her, cleaned up after her, medicated her, and reassured her. And most importantly, loved her and encouraged her.

I did for her what she does for so many others, in another safe place of healing.

Paws for Thought

It literally never ceases to amaze me how profound an impact my sweet, enthusiastic Penny has made on me and almost every aspect of my life.

One of the things I have learned as I have observed her with patients is the importance and value of being totally present in the moment.

This particular morning I settled in my chair to catch the early morning news and to sip my coffee. Penny came up to me and rested her head on my lap to say good morning. As I stroked her soft head and told her how I loved her, she soon melted onto the floor and remained there until I got up to fix her breakfast and prepared to visit the hospital.

As she goes about her daily routine, she is always keenly aware of where I am and what I am doing. She passes no judgments, no criticisms. She is quite simply there.

This was also the case when we met Adam. Adam had been battling cancer at M.D. Anderson. He was now at the rehab hospital after extensive surgery, which left a very large portion of his skull and face missing. As he sat alone in his wheelchair waiting for his therapist, I took a very large breath and approached him smiling. I knew what I had to do. I had to be like Penny. I had to see past the surface and focus on the heart and soul of this man.

This was a strong message. When we see those with a handicap or a disfigurement, we must learn. These people are not defined by their differences, but rather defined by the things that mean the most to them: their family, their values, and their faith. Not unlike the rest of us.

Adam was obviously most appreciative of his meeting with Penny and told her of his life-threatening disease and his struggle. And without words, he told me of his immense courage.

Because of Penny, I have found that there is great wisdom very close to the ground.

"When it hurts to look back and you're afraid to move forward, you can look beside you and your best friend will be there."

— Rachael Hale
Greeting Card

One Visit at a Time

Sometimes we want to fix everything. I have always been questionably blessed with this affliction. But sometimes the only necessary and best action is to just sit still, be present, and do nothing.

Being present, whether for a patient or a loved one. Simply being there. Listening quietly, one patient at a time, one visit at a time.

In college, I had to write an essay on John Milton's quotation from his *Sonnet XIX*. "They also serve who only stand and wait." I struggled then as I do now. The most difficult thing for me is to do nothing.

Penny has reintroduced me to Milton's very valuable lesson of being fully present. By doing so, we are telling a patient, a friend, or a family member that we are there for them.

Now I understand that this is the greatest gift we have to offer. That any of us have to offer. It is at that point that life can truly be celebrated and become real.

So I continue to struggle with the knowledge, and the acceptance, that life is only about now.

Stillness is sometimes all the weary soul needs.

DON'T WAIT

Ruth was about my age when Penny and I first met her. She had been diagnosed with Lou Gehrig's disease (ALS).

At first glance, I was immediately aware of her beautiful brilliant blue eyes, silver gray hair, a flawless complexion, and a smile and dignity from her heart. As she held her hand out to Penny, it was obvious that she had instantly fallen in love with her.

Never taking her eyes off Penny, Ruth struggled to apologize to both of us for not being able to speak well. I told her it didn't matter at all, because we both understood who she was and what she wanted to say from the love in her eyes and from the love reaching out to Penny.

She was grateful that we asked nothing of her. What she had to say to Penny she said through her fingertips and her soul.

I sat quietly as Ruth and this little life-support system "visited." In this moment, quiet time had become a gift.

As I watched, I thought how many people wait to say "I love you."

The lesson learned here was—don't wait.

Don't save it for a special occasion. Each day, each hour, each and every minute is a special occasion.

Refuse to be indifferent.

REDECORATING

When I adopted Penny from Guide Dogs of Texas, I had no way of knowing what she would mean to me and to others or that her mission in life was to become something very special.

The first few days after I adopted her and found we shared the same birthday, I would never have realized how much more we would come to share over the years. Her paperwork never indicated how smart, intuitive, sensitive, and keenly aware this golden retriever with the adoring eyes actually was.

But falling in love with her was not without other blessings.

Ripping up carpets and replacing them with hardwood floors seemed to be a most viable suggestion for Penny and the other dogs. I also discovered that paw prints and nose smudges on my French doors seemed to soften the glare in the room perfectly.

And I don't have to sweep away the little bits of food that fall from the chopping block. The leather furniture looks so much lovelier when textured with Penny's golden hair.

I never have to wear a watch. Penny always makes certain I keep on a tight schedule. No loafing allowed. Breakfast is to be served promptly at 6:30 A.M. and dinner by 5:00 P.M. And I do find the perfect finishing touches to my décor are the doggie beds scattered around the house, adding color and texture, much like designer throw pillows.

But best of all is the feeling of warmth and love that permeates my four walls. Each day is full of surprising and delightful experiences.

I love to decorate. I always wanted the perfect home. My friends all ask me to decorate their homes.

They don't have dogs!

Funny, sometimes I think their homes just don't feel quite right.

> *"We treat our dogs as if they were 'almost human': that is why they really become 'almost human' in the end."*
>
> — C.S. Lewis
> *Mere Christianity*

"Penny by Me"

Sometimes Penny has done her best work with me. Suffering for years from emotional fatigue and depression, I have watched as she has changed the atmosphere wherever she goes. I couldn't figure out why it didn't do the same for me. I had four dogs. If what I had been preaching to others for years was indeed true, why wasn't it working for me? The patients wanted her to visit every day. It seemed to help them. I had her everyday. What was wrong?

Slowly what I came to understand after working with Penny at the rehab hospital was that I had never really trusted before, because when I did, my trust had always been betrayed ever since I was a very little girl.

But it occurred to me quite suddenly one day that I truly trusted this dog. She would not betray me, she would not judge me, and she would never try to control me, manipulate me, or humiliate me.

She would quite simply love me unconditionally. Wow! What a rare, precious gift and revelation. I had trusted her unconditionally with our patients, and now I, too, was able to trust her with my heart.

In training, Penny was taught to understand the command "by me."

This simply meant she was to stay by my left side. Now I understand, on a different level, she is "by me" and I am by her.

We are in this thing together. I had lost my faith, but it had always been right "by me" all along.

How much better can it get?

My heart and soul had been wounded, but my healing process has begun.

I have found the gold ring!

JOSH

Penny had been selected to work privately with an eight-year-old little boy named Josh and his therapist. Josh was extremely hyperactive. His therapist thought perhaps Penny would be able to help calm him.

We first met Josh in the pediatric therapy room and found him racing, running, and talking incessantly. He was on a blue mat with several large brightly colored red and yellow balls. He seemed very interested in Penny and stopped rolling on the balls just long enough to meet her.

His therapist and I asked Josh if he would like to sit quietly and brush Penny. He agreed. Penny curled up on the mat, and Josh cuddled up next to her and sat very still while brushing her back.

Brushing being Penny's favorite thing, she soon fell asleep. Her steady breathing and the gentle brushing also calmed Josh. The therapist spoke softly and slowly, asking him about his pets. Josh seemed pensive and answered quietly.

It didn't seem like a dramatic change had happened. But later his therapist said that that was the biggest change she had seen in Josh.

As we were leaving, he remained calm and asked if Penny could visit with him again.

Twice more we met with Josh, with the same remarkable results.

The last time he told me that he and his family were moving to Georgia, and it would be the last time he would see Penny. To tell Penny good-bye, Josh had drawn a card just for her. It was a picture of him with Penny, a ball, a leash, and a hairbrush.

Under it he wrote, "Penny, I love you. Your friend, Josh."

I gave Josh Penny's photograph. He told me that would be the first thing he would pack to take to his new home.

Josh had made the first step toward learning that sometimes you have to be very still to hear the important things.

"Scratch a dog and you'll find a permanent job."

— Franklin P. Jones

SUNSHINE

It was a quiet day at the hospital. Penny and I were walking down the hallways, visiting with staff and some of the housekeeping crew. The housekeepers had always been so sweet to Penny, offering their sincere smiles to her and wanting to pet her. So this day we stopped to just spend a little time with them.

Her visit sparked comments about their own pets and how they were not nearly as well behaved. I told them how long Penny had been in many, many training classes, and they seemed to understand.

Then one of the housekeepers told me about a "patient down the hall and last on the left" who loved dogs and thought perhaps she would like to meet Penny. What a lovely and kind gesture. I thanked her. Penny and I turned to go visit this patient.

We arrived at her door and the room appeared to be very dark and quite warm. I knocked and asked if she would like a visit with Penny. I heard this sweet voice say, "Oh, yes please."

Esther was dressed in a long red bathrobe pinned with a large, sparkly brooch. She was sitting in her chair at the foot of her bed directly in front of the window. The noon sun was streaming in and framed her silhouette perfectly. She had a very heavy hand knit afghan on her lap and a huge smile on her face. She reached forward and held out both of her hands to Penny. At that moment it was clear all she wanted in the entire world was to touch Penny and cradle her face in her hands.

As she touched Penny, she told me how much she loved dogs and missed having any. She asked all about Miss Penny. How old was she? How long had she been a therapy dog? How had she gotten her name? We simply sat and had a very lovely peaceful visit. She told me how much she appreciated my taking the time to just sit with her and for bringing Penny.

In a busy hospital, people run in and out of the rooms, but seldom do they have the time to just be present for a patient, to just sit and be.

If I didn't understand the meaning of life at the hospital, the rest would be meaningless. To be truly present for someone is the greatest gift you can give.

"One reason a dog can be such a comfort when you're feeling blue is that he doesn't try to find out why."

— Author Unknown

PANCAKES

Penny and I had been working with a young patient for about ten minutes. Allen was taking small dog treats and laboriously putting them one by one into the hole in Penny's Kong™ ball.

Practicing this manual dexterity was tiring. So we took a little break and Allen quietly began to pet Penny's head. He moved one finger carefully between her eyes and up to the top of her head. I unfolded his other fingers and placed his open hand back on her head. He let it sit there for a few seconds when Penny gave him a little nudge. He got the message.

Allen had great trouble keeping his fingers straight and not letting them curl under. But all of a sudden I noticed he was holding her ear and then, with his fingers outstretched, he began feeling her ear with very deliberate, slow movements.

The silence was broken with one word "pancake." I thought perhaps I had not heard correctly. So I said I was sorry, but I didn't hear what he had said. He repeated, "pancake."

It took a while, but I finally understood. He was telling me that her soft ears reminded him of pancakes, the shape, the softness, the color.

I gave Allen a big hug and said I would never forget him and Penny and her "pancake" ears.

He smiled.

My day was perfect!

There had been a tiny miracle around the corner.

MY DESK

Sometimes blessings are disguised in pain. It is hard to believe at the time, but nonetheless most often true.

I had been told to "journal" to get my feelings out. "Write it down, tear if up, and throw it away. Let it go! Only time will heal you."

But the solitude of writing Penny's stories, and the hours in the quiet of my office brought about a kind of healing with a depth I could never have expected.

The top of my desk contains things that I love. A photograph by artist Henry Holdsworth of a pile of seven-week-old sleeping golden retriever puppies ("Puppy Pile") that I got in Jackson, Wyoming, a beautiful crystal lead paperweight from Santa Fe that I can stare at and get lost in, an antique English wooden and brass letter holder that reminds me of a trip with my stepdad to The Cotswalds, my daughter's baby picture, a seashell from the Gulf of Mexico, Anne Morrow Lindberg's *Gifts from the Sea,* a rice bowl from my year in Korea, a framed needlepoint canvas of a special dog friend from my past, and a canvas bag full of tiny inspirational books, a sand dollar, and special photographs of sunsets and sunrises are all part of who I am. Memories, peaceful precious memories of other places and times.

I like to have them on my desk while I write. They remind me of what is important to me, as well as what isn't. They are things that remain and tie me to this earth.

Writing has been my friend as I have plowed through days of grief and despair. I have desperately wanted to convey in writing the beauty of this incredible partnership with Penny. Ironically, I believe I have wanted to do that way before Penny was born. I hope it makes sense when I say that I just didn't know it yet.

With Penny by my side, I have witnessed smiles, tears, and struggles of patients, their friends, and loved ones. This has deeply affected my own life.

My emotional energy had been depleted; the framework of my life had crumbled and when I needed a rope to hang onto, writing and Penny were there.

And now as I write at my desk of memories, I have a new feeling.

I feel something new is coming, something full of wonder and excitement. I can't tell you what it is, but I can tell you it is coming.

Now I must listen intently to what has been trying to speak through me.

There are many lessons to be learned from the blessings of pain.

"We will be known forever by the tracks we leave."
— Dakota-Native American Proverb

Moments

There are moments with Penny and her patients that I want to save, to remember, to write down and cherish. But often a new moment appears before I get to paper and pen. Another and then another incredible moment happen, interrupting the writing process.

And then I remember this isn't about me, and it isn't about this book or even Penny. It is about the moments. Whether they get written down or remembered doesn't really matter.

What does matter is that they happened.

Gifts

Everyone's gifts are different. My gift back to the world is what one person described as "fulfilling my destiny" and "finding my purpose." As remarkable as it may sound, I agree. I am so deeply blessed to have found a niche that truly makes my heart sing.

All of my friends are different with different gifts. Each one offers something uniquely their own. One listens, one offers great wisdom, one makes me laugh, one brings food and flowers, and one takes me shopping. Each one of their gifts is a cherished treasure of a beautiful friendship.

My friends have helped heal my hurt each in their own wonderful unique ways. Never judging me, just loving me.

Isn't this exactly what Penny has done for her patients? She has no ego, no plan, no agenda. It isn't all about *her*.

With her passionate, joyful spirit, she never judges or makes comments under her breath; she just loves. Quiet times with Penny have become the ultimate gift.

In these times, I understand that people who have experienced great pain and struggles are, on an emotional and spiritual level, much more than they were before: more compassionate, more sensitive, more loving, and more aware of the immense beauty in the smallest things.

It is a secret that you want to share, but you just can't. People must learn this for themselves by stepping back and quite simply paying attention.

"One can never creep when one feels an impulse to soar."

— Helen Keller

The Best Surprise Ever

For almost a year, Fred was unable to speak or move or lift his head.

Each week Penny visited with him, and he always managed some small recognition of her presence.

This day, Penny was back at the hospital after a very long six weeks off due to a hot spot that would not heal. Everyone turned and looked, waved and said, "Oh, Penny is back." To me it was like being offered a glass of water when you are very, very thirsty.

We saw Fred in the hall with his wife heading to speech therapy. I was so pleased to see that he was looking alert, his eyes bright and cheerful. He was dressed beautifully and smelled slightly of cologne. As always his wife said, "Fred, here's Penny." But this time she had a funny little secretive look on her face. We were quite unexpectedly presented with an incredible gift—the best surprise ever.

Fred looked at us and said, "Hi Penny!"

I am seldom at a loss for words, but I know I must have stood there totally speechless for a minute or longer. I looked at his wife in amazement, and she told me that one morning he just woke up speaking. She told me the date and the exact hour and minute. "There was no good reason for it; it was a miracle."

Fred had had a brain aneurysm. A very large portion of his skull had been removed while the swelling reduced in his brain. The portion of the skull was returned and recovery from that was long and slow. But each time I saw Fred, his wife was right next to him and always she was touching him. She made sure he retained his dignity no matter what. She combed his hair, saw that his clothing was immaculate and that he was shaved and smelled good.

Recovery was hard work. With expert medical care, time, patience, perseverance and love, Fred would recover.

Love, faith, hope, and believing with all their hearts was the miracle.

Today I learned to never forget where you put a dream.

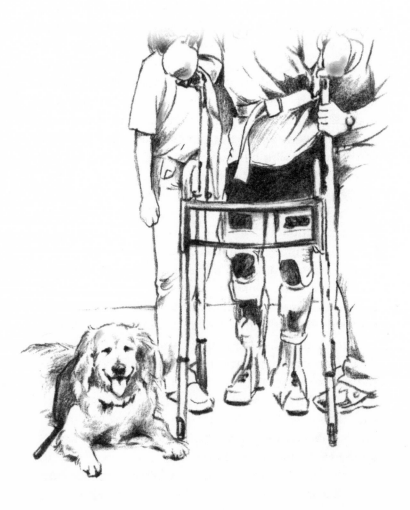

SPOONS

Valerie was lying on a raised mat doing leg lifts. Her therapist close by, Valerie appeared to be in pain. She had at one time been told she would never walk again and to "accept it." She said "No, I won't accept it. I will walk again."

She is now an outpatient and is home with her three kids and a Labrador puppy. She finds it exhausting to even put water in a pan to boil hot dogs for the kids. But she never complains and knows it will take time. She does not settle for less than being back to normal.

Valerie does therapy most of each day. And the progress she has made is dramatic. From being bedridden, to a wheelchair, to a walker, and now a cane, Valerie is tenacious in her pursuit of being a full-time mom to her three children. But in the meantime, the children have learned to help her.

"They pick up their rooms, they help with meals and they take care of each other and even do their homework without being told," Valerie said.

She and I talked while she was doing her leg exercises, partially to take her mind off of the pain. While we were talking, Penny had jumped up on the mat, snuggled in close to Valerie and laid her head on her shoulder. Soon 70-pound Penny turned over onto her back and managed to get her head on the same pillow.

Everyone in the gym was pointing and saying, "Look at Penny."

Soon visitors, patients, and therapists were surrounding the mat.

All were smiling at this special furry therapist that seemed to be totally in charge.

The therapist asked Valerie to turn onto her side. Soon she and Penny were "spoons," once again sharing the same pillow. Valerie wrapped her arm around Penny, continued to do her leg exercises, and told Miss Penny that her day was so much better because of her visit. Other patients agreed and wanted some of Penny's special medicine.

In the gentleness of Penny's soul, other patients were finding peace in the midst of pain.

"The truly wise person kneels at the feet of all creatures."
— Mechtild of Madgeburg

HOPE

Shari had been thrown from a horse and was admitted for therapy for a closed head injury. This was her first day in rehab. Her mom and cousin had intercepted Penny and me as we were leaving the hospital. They explained Shari had horses, dogs, cats, and all kinds of critters at home and that she would love to have a visit from Penny. They appeared almost apologetic and embarrassed to ask.

We went to her room, and Shari seemed somewhat pleased to see Penny. She petted her briefly and returned her hand to her lap, asking her mom if her pets at home were being cared for.

Her mom and cousin were elated to learn about Penny's hospital duties. Almost in tears, her mom explained to me how much animals meant to Shari. Her life had always been geared around them. She had just been starting work with her horses to train them to be used as equestrian therapy horses when this freak accident occurred.

I shared several stories of Penny's patients in the hospital, and they felt a sense of optimism and hope. I explained how wonderful the hospital staff was and how great the therapists were with the patients. Penny offered hope. We left the room with promises to return soon.

We watched over the next several weeks as Penny opened Shari to joy, sorrow, comfort, and many emotions she had suppressed and long forgotten.

Shari is now home with her horses, dogs, and cats and a new knowledge of what pet therapy can truly accomplish.

There is a time for gratefulness.

A Candle

I have always loved candles and found watching them to be so peaceful. It seems to relax me, as I become mesmerized by the flickering flame. Amazing how just one candle is able to make such an incredible difference.

I sometimes think of my Penny as one candle, a candle that makes a huge difference, sometimes only to one patient, one life, one at a time. Over and over again I see a peace come over a patient that is hard to express in words. It is in their eyes, and I often sense that it goes to their soul.

Not everyone who meets Penny is moved to this extent, but it doesn't need to be everyone. It is enough if it is just one.

There is a purpose for us here, identifying with another's journey.

Even through a candle, life can be talking to you. It is up to you to listen.

"Don't walk in front of me; I might not follow. Don't walk behind me; I might not lead. Just walk beside me and be my friend."

— Albert Camus

THE NEW FRIEND

Thanksgiving morning. I needed to do something meaningful.

Penny and I got ready to go to the hospital and see whatever patients had not been released to go home for the day.

We arrived and found the gym was locked, so we started walking by one room at a time. Most of the patients were gone, but a few remained.

One gentleman in his wheelchair in the hall instantly adored Penny. He held her head in his hands. "This is the best medicine of all today. Thank you, oh thank you," he said.

Another lady began crying and telling me how much our visit had meant to her. Her family was far away, and she had no one coming to see her. She told me how sad she was that Thanksgiving is most often overlooked.

"The stores are open for Christmas sales on Thanksgiving." She wanted me to know that Thanksgiving, at least to her, was "the most special day of all. I have so much to be thankful for. I am so blessed. The sacrifices the pilgrims made means everything to me." Tears came to her eyes, and I knew what she meant.

Without knowing her circumstances, I understood. She had a room in a wonderful hospital, a pillow to lay her head on, and a visit from Penny, a new friend.

Penny wedged her head through the sidebars of the bed to lay her head next to this lady, whose name I don't know. It didn't matter.

To Penny she was a nice person who simply wanted to pet her, and to me she was someone who knew the meaning of Thanksgiving in the truest sense.

She spoke gently to Penny. As she did so, Penny's eyes closed to rest and absorb the attention.

Thanksgiving should be a lifestyle, not just one day a year.

"A faithful friend is the medicine of life."
— Unknown

Two Little Girls

Sitting in the waiting room of the pet hospital on a Saturday morning, Penny made friends instantly with two little girls, one seven and one five. Penny has been trained to lie on her side around children and allow them to pet her, lie beside her, or simply stroke her fur.

These little girls were so animated and thrilled with meeting Penny. They immediately sat on the floor next to her and asked many, many questions. I told them that Penny was sort of like a nurse. "She visits sick people in the hospital." Amazingly they both seemed to get it.

Their mother, totally without expression, was holding their dog and appeared completely disinterested in her daughters, as well as in Penny. The five year old said with phenomenal enthusiasm, "Oh Mommy, Mommy, this is Penny and she is a nurse. She goes to the hospital and visits sick people to make them better." The mother ignored her and picked up her cell phone to make a call.

I sat quietly wondering how two such precious children with obviously beautiful, vibrant personalities came to be the way they were despite it all.

Maybe just maybe they will remember Penny and some day take their own dogs to visit "sick people in the hospital to make them better."

"Friends are like quiet angels, they pick you up when your wings have forgotten how to fly."
— Unknown

POINSETTIAS

I had the strangest sense of springtime this one morning. It was only four days until New Year's Eve. The weather was beautifully warm at 64 degrees. The Christmas closet was cleaned, the boxes ready for Goodwill pickup, files ready for the accountant, and clothes that no longer fit placed in a sad little pile. Proof that the Christmas chocolate was yummy!

Even Penny had a spring in her step and an outlook for fun every moment. She was ready. She wasn't sure what she was ready for, but she was ready.

She watched as I pulled out the potting soil from the garage to fill clay pots and begin planting scavenged poinsettias that nobody wanted any longer. It always seems somewhat sad that they give their very best, dressed in their Christmas red, white, and salmon colors, to be placed on the curb for trash pickup when the first leaf falls off. They gave their best, only to be thrown away.

I have always tried to save some of them, the same way I have tried to save all too few dogs and cats. It makes me think of the millions of sad little dogs and cats that are discarded yearly for simply being alive and a nuisance to their owners. For lack of a little discipline, nurturing, and love, they are not unlike the poinsettias. Discarded for no reason other than they are no longer cute or convenient.

It is my hope that after reading this book, people will take a second and a third look at the overwhelming potential and awesome inspiration that is built into each little four-footed furry critter.

They then might not be so quick to discard them on the curb like rubbish.

Unpaved Roads

It was hot—88 degrees. It was the middle of November. Heat records were being broken here in South Texas. Sweaters are still packed away. I was at the car dealership waiting on repairs—it's said a writer can write anywhere.

But whatever the weather, it is that time of year we set aside for giving thanks. It seems we all want and are thankful for the big things that set us apart, or help us keep up with the frantic life we tend to thrive on, or to keep up with the Joneses, or perhaps simply make us feel more important.

Do we ever settle down and appreciate the little things we are blessed with everyday? A flag blowing in the breeze shouting out "freedom," a plant growing in a sidewalk crack struggling to reach the sun, a very old couple holding hands, a little boy clinging to his grandpa's finger to cross the street, a kindness from a total stranger.

Then there is the look in the face of one of Penny's patients as they watch her put her head in their laps no matter what their illness or how they look, giving her precious gift, asking nothing in return.

Growing up, Thanksgiving was a big deal. The good china, silver, and crystal came out of hiding twice a year and was polished and suitably admired. The table set, the meal prepared, people seated, prayers said, and then the ooohs and ahhhs over the turkey—naps taken and then nibbling on leftovers.

One Thanksgiving was different and my most memorable. Penny and I went to a nursing home. It was about 11 AM and the lunch trays were being delivered. Turkey, dressing, and cranberries filled the plates and of course there was pumpkin pie.

I was so grateful to be there because it truly broke my heart to see the patients dining alone. No family, no friends to sit with most of them. No good china or celebration. It was simply another day and another meal alone.

Penny and I made our way down the halls to as many patients as we could to say "Happy Thanksgiving" and to offer some companionship while they ate.

They all seemed to appreciate that we cared enough to give our time to interrupt their loneliness.

Someone sent me a joke once, "Some people try to turn back their clock, not me. I want people to know 'why' I look this way. I've traveled a long way and some of the roads weren't paved."

I am thankful for those unpaved roads, for people, days, hours, minutes, blessings, love, life, puppy dogs, health, children, grandchildren, little things—big things.

You see, some rocky roads are more painful than others. But we learn what is ultimately important and what is not.

"The stories people tell have a way of taking care of them. If stories come to you, care for them. And learn to give them away where they are needed. Sometimes a person needs a story more than food to stay alive."

— Barry Lopez
Crow and Weasel

Standing Vigil

I had been in a hurry. I was late and needed to be in my car and on the way to an appointment. But the dogs were outside and refused to come in. I made one last trip to the door to call them and promptly tripped over a two-inch step and landed on the side of my foot.

I heard and felt the bone break. Ironically, that was when all four dogs came in as I called a friend to drive me to the doctor's office.

Within thirty minutes I was being x-rayed. Yes, my foot was broken in three places.

Oh boy! Living alone in a two-story house with crutches and a badly broken foot. This was going to be challenging. No bedrooms downstairs. How would I manage with the dogs wanting in and out and my office being upstairs?

But surprisingly the healing process, although quite painful, afforded me time to slow down. It took twenty minutes just to climb the stairs. Ms. Gourmet's dinner became peanut butter sandwiches and canned soup.

Amazingly, or perhaps not so amazing, Penny rose to the occasion and remembered her guide dog training. She stood to my left going up and down the steps very slowly one at a time. She sensed my pain, and she stood vigilant. Somehow understanding.

She was cautious of the crutches and later the cane, being careful not to get too near. She slept extra close by the side of my bed.

Late at night I felt her get up frequently. She would place her head on the bed close to me and simply watch me.

In reflection, this had been a time of slowing down to recognize the beauty around me. It had been a time to watch and emulate my dogs' lives of simplicity. If I was hungry I would eat, if sleepy I would sleep, and sometimes I'd just lie and watch a movie.

It was a time when I found what was closest to my soul. A time when I found that whatever else needed doing could wait.

THE FLOOR

When I was young, my mother would not allow me to walk in certain rooms of our house. It was where I lived, but it was definitely not a home.

Goldie, our housekeeper, (mother called her the maid) would come to clean. Once she vacuumed, no one in the family was allowed to walk in the dining room or the living room. I never quite understood this, finding it very strange. But it was simple to mother. The tracks from the vacuum were not to be disturbed. And if they were, I would be punished. I remember thinking that I couldn't wait to get my own home.

Today my house is a place where the floor, quite simply, makes it a home. You will find paw prints, leaves, twigs, faux suede dog beds, kibbles of dog food, water bowls, stuffed and unstuffed toys, and my sleeping, contented best friends.

Penny, Gracie, Lulu, and Wally will all watch patiently when I vacuum, sweep, and mop.

I am certain they must be wondering why I find it necessary to perform this useless ritual. But no worries, they know that soon, tails wagging, they will begin fixing the floor. Once again, they will scatter leaves and toys, just like they scatter love and sunshine throughout the hospital.

Today on my floor you will learn about love and find footprints that will remain in your heart.

"For everything there is a season and a time for every matter under heaven."

— Ecclesiastes 3:1

MARIO

Mario was a spunky, courageous young man who, while asleep, received a gunshot to the head from a "friend." This is what he told me with help from his computer. He had a love for Penny that wouldn't end. His eyes would light up across the room, and you could hear him calling her, "Hey, hey!"

Mario couldn't talk, but his computer could tell you about his accident, his parents, what food he liked, his family, and his pets.

He was so proud when he got the computer attached to his wheelchair so that he could tell people who he was. He gleamed as he punched buttons that seemingly illuminated his life.

As he clicked on "Pets," there came Penny's name. I told him I was delighted that he had adopted Penny as his dog, too. Mario proudly shared this with everyone as he petted Penny and rubbed her ears.

Why is it we often seem to applaud the unimportant things and make the important things unimportant?

"Today is 'golden,' for today is here, and you are here to fill it with your own unique value. Today you can, if you will."

— Ralph Marston
Daily Motivator

SOMEONE TO WATCH OVER ME

I find that when I think of only myself or my problems, the answer almost always is to find someone to help.

Sometimes that help takes different guises. More often than not, that help comes, and only can come, from within. It could simply be a quick trip to buy a new pair of shoes, get a haircut, or have lunch with a friend. But the best help of all is being able to enjoy and love yourself.

For the pain of betrayal that was perpetrated upon me, I am now eternally grateful. What an amazing surprise! I am finally complete; I am fulfilled. I feel blessed and brimming with gratitude for every single moment I am alive. First and foremost I am grateful for me. The person I am. The person I have become.

This deep feeling of gratitude is one of the ultimate joys of my life. It will not evaporate or vanish. It arrived in a moment of grace, and it will stay.

Lack of gratitude "decays the spirit, spoils the soul, and decomposes life itself," according to Lewis B. Smedes in *A Pretty Good Person.* "Life calls us to gratitude the way the sun says to the buried seed: 'You ought to break out of your shell and come alive as the lovely flower you were always meant to be.'"

Betrayal, the struggle through the pain I could not control, and the journey to heal from it, a step at a time, became a gift. The gift of a new life, where I am now the flower I was always meant to be.

Sitting at the computer with Penny sleeping a single step away, I get it. I understand. And I stand ready to do whatever is in my power to help others understand. Without Penny I don't know that this would have happened.

Someone was watching over me. It doesn't get any better than this. For this I am blessed and, for the grace of Penny, perhaps one day others will be able to celebrate their pain and their imperfections.

"A friend is someone with whom we can relax and just hang out, have fun and share our innermost thoughts – deep dark secrets, lofty and noble goals, or our hopes, joys and fears. A good friend allows you a safe space for feeling the way you do."
— Bettie and Jennifer Leigh Youngs
Taste Berries for Teens

THE DOGSLED ADVENTURE
— A LIFE STORY —

As far back as I can remember, I had wanted to take a dogsled trip. One Christmas my daughter, Kim, who lives in Montana, surprised me with a pair of pink snow goggles and a gift certificate for my dream come true.

I had beautiful romantic notions of how it would be. The sun would be shining on sparkling snow. The adventure would be slow paced, peaceful, and quiet.

Two days later, my daughter and son-in-law and I began our journey at 11,000 feet, high in the Montana wilderness. It was 16 degrees below zero.

Being a Texas gal, I must have looked like a little girl in a snowsuit going out to play, hardly able to walk for all the layers of clothes. But my anticipation was keen.

We signed the waiver, listened to instructions, and then I settled into the sled with my daughter. My son-in-law Paul volunteered to be the "musher." We were the third sled in a group of six, each sled having twelve dogs. Some were retired Iditarod dogs, some huskies, and some mixed breeds. All of them were excited to do what they instinctively do and straining "to go."

The high-pitched bark indicated that "lift off" was close. Within just seconds, the first sled took off and the second and then ours.

I was energized and excited as I sat with my legs straight out, with my daughter behind me. The snow was blowing in our faces from the racing dogs and the wind was making sharp little pinpricks of icy pain on our faces.

There was nothing between us and the hard-packed snow, except the canvas stretched between the runners.

I grabbed my camera to capture the moment of racing through this pristine snow-covered meadow, beneath the tallest snow-dressed pines I had ever seen. It was straight out of a Currier and Ives painting.

As I watched the dogs running, they would duck their heads into the snow with their mouths open to take in moisture. I thought of my Texas four-legged critters fast asleep, resting up for dinner.

This dogsled ride began as everything I had hoped it would be. Suddenly I saw the sled in front of us on a very sheer ledge against the mountain and a drop straight down that made me catch my breath. I recalled the waiver I signed. I said a little prayer and remembered this was my dream to take this trip. It would be okay.

As we rounded the mountain, both my daughter and I leaned toward the mountain and avoided looking down the hundred or more feet on the other side.

One misstep by one dog would have caused a disaster. But soon we came out of the mountain into another meadow. I was feeling better and took a deep breath.

Then quite suddenly we hit "the rock." Paul was instantly thrown from the sled. Our musher was gone (we were afraid down the mountain).

We were on a runaway dogsled with literally no way to stop the team.

We couldn't see the sled behind or in front of us. All I could think to do was yell "help." As we rounded the next curve, we found the guide had heard me and had stopped his team. He was yelling to us "you're okay, you're okay." Funny, I didn't feel okay.

Our runaway team was forced to stop instantly as they plowed into the team of twelve dogs in front of us. Twenty-four dogs ended up in a pile with our dogsled, my daughter, and me on top.

Both teams of dogs were struggling frantically to get free. Ropes and legs were intertwined. From our perch on top of the dogs, we were desperate to find out what had happened to Paul. We strained to look back when we saw another sled come up behind us with him on it. Paul jumped off the sled and helped us out of our sled while the two guides pulled it off the dogs and began to separate the masses of frightened dogs that were all knotted together.

Miraculously none were seriously injured. We changed teams with the guide and resumed the journey…a little worse for wear. And needless to say, our enthusiasm was definitely gone.

It wasn't too much further when we were told a tree was on the trail, and we had to move the team closer to the edge of the cliff to get the dogs to the left of it. The drop was a long one. My dream continued to be shattered. What next?

As we approached the fallen tree, it was obvious the dogs were in control and not us. Six dogs went on one side of the tree and six to the other side. The guide once again pulled the dogs apart and "righted" the sled. Off we went for another 20 minutes before stopping for hot chocolate and chocolate chip cookies. Brandy sounded better.

We were battered, bruised, and tired. Suffice it to say, the joy had been taken out of the trip, and we all had become quite reluctant to continue. But there was no other choice. I was trying to keep a "happy face" for my daughter since it was her not so inexpensive Christmas gift to me…and it was her birthday!

The guides asked if we were doing okay, and if we wanted to take the long or short way back to base camp. What a question. Short it was.

So in ten more minutes we were back. Kim and Paul went to the truck. I went back to the sled to find my lens cap to my camera. As I did, I overheard our guide tell a friend, "Well, we hit that darn rock again." I couldn't believe what I heard. I calmly, with as much grace as I could muster, asked why they didn't just "move the rock." No answer.

I came back to Texas and was telling a friend about the dogsled adventure. I was waiting for sympathy as she listened intently. But I didn't get any. She said it sounded a lot like life. We start out full of joy, anticipation, and excitement. Everything goes along great for a while, then you hit a rock—a big rock and the setback is upsetting and unsettling and makes you a little apprehensive of going forward. Your choice is to quit or keep on going.

You calm down, enjoy the ride, and then complacency sets in, and you hit another rock. Same thing again.

It isn't about how many rocks you hit. It is about how you handle hitting them. Do you let them ruin the journey or do you accept them for what they are and go on, knowing there will be another time and another rock. And with each rock you learn. You learn you can take it. You learn you can go on. You grow from it and learn how strong you really are.

Then one day you look back and realize what the experience brought to you.

You look at it with fresh eyes. You see it is just life.

You get some good. You get some bad. At times it is scary. You go on.

You forgive. Eventually you forget. The pain gets less from the rocks you hit.

We nurture and are nurtured. Sometimes we're offered hot chocolate and chocolate chip cookies.

Life is always talking to you. It is up to you to listen and to pay attention.

Sometimes we have hopes and dreams, and sometimes they are shattered.

Like Penny's patients we all move forward one step at a time, one hurdle at a time.

"Life is like a dogsled team. If you ain't the lead dog, the scenery never changes."

— Lewis Grizzard

A LOVE STORY

At a dog show, I met a lovely lady, ironically, named Penny, with her beautiful Great Pyrenees, Dakota. I was drawn to them initially because he was such a gorgeous "Pyr" and I, too, am owned by one. But the real answer as to my interest was just beginning to unfold.

I stood back for a while and watched as her husband groomed Dakota on a large elevated table just prior to his showing. Nothing seemed to make this ordinary moment special, until I saw Dakota's "dad" gently lower his forehead to meet the dog's beautiful white muzzle and coal black nose. It was as if there was no one else in the world. This position was held for a few seconds, as he kissed the top of Dakota's muzzle with such love and affection that I felt I was somehow intruding simply by watching. This seemingly unimportant routine grooming changed into an instant love story and a powerful moment in time, full of incredible beauty and devotion.

Penny told me that they weren't breeders. They quite simply truly loved their dogs and wanted to share them proudly with others. To them it wasn't important whether they won or not. It seems Dakota is also a therapy dog and is widely sought after in Plano, Texas to minister with his own "stories of healing."

We talked about pet therapy for a few minutes and then she told me "some dog show folks simply have dogs for ribbons and awards." But lucky Dakota! His "mom and dad" told me that the best part of being loved by Dakota is that at the end of the day he goes home with them and is their dog.

Sometimes words are just inadequate to define love. But a forehead and a big white muzzle can tell a great deal about the truest, simplest kind of love.

I feel Leo Buscaglia said it best. "Don't miss love. It's an incredible gift." He felt that the day we are born, we are given the world as a birthday present, and it frightened him that so few people bother to open up the gift. "Rip it open! Tear off the top! It's just full of love and magic and life and joy and wonder and pain and tears."

I hurried home to a golden muzzle and a brown nose. Penny seemed to understand.

She, too, is love.

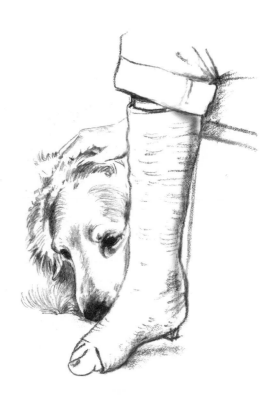

Sometimes

Sometimes when you need it the most, a friend, an event, or a circumstance comes along. Sometimes it could be in the guise of a four-footed friend, it could be a kind word from a stranger, an encouraging word from an attorney, or a doctor, or a friend from years past who called "just thinking about you," or perhaps simply finding yourself in the right place at the right time.

However it comes, you will know it. No criticism will be offered.

No resentment. No judgment. Friendships are given freely and exercised freely, as are courage and compassion.

Mary Anne Radmacher has a wonderful quotation, "Courage doesn't always roar. Sometimes courage is the quiet voice at the end of the day saying, 'I will try again tomorrow.'"

We have all been there. For me courage comes from writing.

Writing from the soul. When I write I am living in the moment, where love, passion, and compassion become one. Time passes, pain passes, and amazement and wonder step in. Writing is my escape hatch.

This day I planned to write about Penny. But I was having nagging unresolved conflicts in my mind and decided to spend the day with her instead. Nothing I could write would be as important as offering her my time. All too often we become consumed by seemingly urgent things. Our identity is temporarily twisted by our own sense of self-importance and our need to control outcomes. How stupid to think we are that worthy.

A friend called this morning. Aware of my inward struggle, he told me to "just let it go." I gave him a very sincere thank you and told him that "after a good cry I would feel better." He understood and told me "that sometimes helps."

But quite suddenly, grace made a giant leap into the dynamics of the situation and almost instantly my heart-beat slowed as I took a deep breath.

I knew I didn't need to cry. What I needed to do, without consideration, was to leave the office and head to the nursery and pick up some lovely, fresh spring flowers. Simply selecting the plants was nourishment for my soul.

I went home and Penny and I began planting pink, yellow, and white flowered plants on this especially warm sunny March day.

The birds watched, and the doves cooed almost romantically to each other. The sun felt good on my skin, and I could have sworn I heard Puccini somewhere in the background as a plane passed overhead. We were preparing for a fresh start as we watered and fertilized these symbols of rebirth. Penny was facing retirement, and I was facing a blessed future full of great promise. It was a good day after all.

I was quietly reminded of what my friend Terry Hershey had written in *Sacred Necessities.* "See that bearded iris? That is not just a flower, it's smelling-salts for the soul."

It was a joyful day. It reminded me that sometimes you just have to help yourself by listening and paying close attention. When you slow down and really listen to the much-needed silence inside of you, the need for participation in frivolous, insignificant things that are out of your control ceases.

Joy steps in and your need to control, quite suddenly is overcome by an overwhelmingly beautiful infatuation with life.

If you lose yourself in a seemingly inconsequential moment, I assure you that you will find it is therapy for your soul.

Listen to the animals.

Observe.

"Nobody has ever measured, not even poets, how much the heart can hold."

— Zelda Fitzgerald

THE CHRISTMAS CACTUS

This particular patient had been in Hurricane Katrina in New Orleans. Thomas had buried his mother a week before the flood, and a week later he had the first of two strokes. He had always been a favorite of Penny's and mine. He had fought and fought and had improved dramatically since we first saw him months ago.

And now he was waiting to go home…back to New Orleans.

His "home had been gutted and full of mold," Thomas told me as Penny slept at his feet. Every now and then she would glance up to make sure I was still there. She would wag her tail and take a deep breath and go back to sleep. My girl was getting tired.

He told me of his friends trying to repair his roof in time for his homecoming. He still had no furniture. And he softly told me how he missed his mother.

Tears started to well up in his eyes. Penny somehow was aware of this and, as if listening to the conversation, her eyes started moving from our patient to me and back again. The more emotion that was released, the more concern Penny showed. He began telling Penny of his own dog. He didn't remember her name, but he had gotten her because she had one blue eye.

Soon Penny's head was in Thomas' lap. Thomas began scratching her ears, in a beautiful moment of grace. We all remained silent for a few minutes, lost in our own thoughts.

Soon two of his family members arrived with a potted Christmas cactus.

He dried his eyes so no one would notice. Just before Penny and I were ready to leave, he told me his cactus would bloom at Christmas. He would be home with his blue-eyed dog. He was sorry he couldn't remember her name.

I was reminded of what Lewis B. Smedes said in *A Pretty Good Person*.

> *"Walking on this journey sometimes we get very sad. There are abundant reasons for decent people to surrender to their sorrow. And when people dig into the strength and rise to unsung moments of courage, sometimes the only way they have to explain it is that they love life too much to surrender to death."*

What a beautiful word—*courage*.

WHERE DO YOU GO TO DEAL WITH YOUR PAIN?

We had been visiting with patients for at least an hour and a half, and I knew Penny was tired. But there are always the patients who haven't been able to see her. I feel guilty leaving, but I know many times Penny has nothing else to give. This is the hardest part.

Steve, a small framed man in a wheelchair, asked as we were leaving if Penny could sit on his lap. I explained Penny really wasn't allowed to do that and that she was a bit too large.

He then asked if he could "lie down on a mat and just feel her warmth." This was hard to refuse. His therapist helped him onto the mat, and I gave Penny the "up" command. She lay down next to Steve, cuddled up real close, and in just a few moments fell asleep with her head on his pillow.

Sometimes words are unnecessary. Sometimes you just watch and absorb the moment.

Steve changed. His furrowed forehead relaxed, his eyes softened, his pain lessened, and tears came. A strong man battered by life, at least for a while, melted as he found great comfort and peace in the arms of a golden miracle. It was as if his heart didn't feel so broken anymore.

Steve said "Sometimes you just need to lay your burden down."

"There is a sacredness in tears. They are not the mark of weakness, but of power. They speak more eloquently than ten thousand tongues. They are the messengers of overwhelming grief, or deep contrition, and of unspeakable love."

— Washington Irving

THE DOG THAT WAS SORRY

I immediately thought this patient very closely resembled the actress Betty White. I wasn't alone. She said everyone thought she did, too. She was beautiful.

It seems she was in rehab for a broken hip. "I broke my hip when I tripped and fell over my dog." Her eyes were twinkling, and she was smiling as she told Penny and me the story. She then, almost apologetically, made it very clear that she was quite certain her dog was terribly sorry.

Her family was insistent that she "get rid of the dog." But she stood firm. "I wouldn't trade anything for my dog. There is no one or anything that loves me like that."

I understood.

"Dogs provide an uncomplicated, affection-on-demand relationship....Animals add richness and joy to our lives. They reintroduce spontaneity and laughter to our over-structured days. Thanks to animals, we are more compassionate, less hurried, and more willing to share. Pets add years to our lives and life to our years."

Skeeter RX Therapy Team
Skeeter Training Guide

SILENT SYMPATHY

There is great freedom to be who you are in the presence of a dog.

Often Penny puts people in a mood to talk. But there are times a patient will sit silently and simply stroke her soft fur.

Such was the case with Charlotte. We were about ready to end one of our visits when a therapist came rushing to us. "We have an emergency," she said. "Come quickly!"

Penny and I changed course and turned to see a young woman not much more than 25 years old sitting all alone trembling and crying unashamedly. Penny and I approached her. I put my arms around her and asked her what all these tears were. Penny simply laid her head in Charlotte's lap. Nothing was said except that she missed her dogs.

I understood. I sat down next to her and just let her feel what she was feeling, without interruption. In a few moments, Charlotte began to lift her paralyzed left arm across her body with her right hand. She placed her left hand on Penny's head and held it securely with her right hand. Her tears were flowing as she said with such an incredible depth of emotion, "It feels so good to feel her fur."

Charlotte was experiencing great emotional liberation in Penny's presence. And Penny, as if to say she understood, saluted this young woman's strength and courage by lifting her right paw and placing it carefully on Charlotte's lap.

Sometimes when tears come, it means your soul is talking.

THE WORLD STOOD STILL

For months, Penny had been visiting a lady school teacher who had been seriously injured by a drunk driver. Her severe head injuries resulted in multiple surgeries, and she had permanent vision loss in one eye. For every visit, Judy would simply stare into space while she petted Penny.

I would visit with her as if she could hear me. I would tell her all about Penny and her adventures that week. There had never been the slightest recognition until this one magnificent day.

With her husband close by, I was sitting beside Judy on the elevated mat. I talked to both of them and told them that Penny had been to the doctor and might be facing another cancer surgery.

Without hesitation, Judy's forehead wrinkled and she reached for Penny and began stroking her and exhibiting great concern. She appeared agitated. The therapist told me this was "good, very good." Judy had understood what I told her— a giant step in the healing process.

I took Judy's hand and put my arm around her shoulder. I told her how proud I was of her achievements and what an incredible woman she was. I told her not to worry, Penny was a cancer survivor, and she would survive this time as well. I told her they were both survivors.

Judy, for the first time, tracked Penny with her eyes and seemed to relax and understand.

For that moment, Penny, with gentleness in her soul, made the world take pause.

Golden sunshine!

WAITING

Penny had been panting excessively off and on for weeks, losing hair and drinking much too much water. I called the doctor and he wanted to run tests.

So this cloudy hot day, I took Penny to get blood tests to determine whether or not she had Cushing's disease. She hated being left at the animal hospital for the two hours it would take. I hated leaving her. She was afraid. I could sense it.

I drove around doing senseless errands to make the time go faster.

I returned to pick her up in two hours. She came tearing out of the exam room like her life depended upon it. She lunged into my lap, and off we went to the car. I gave her a granola bar, and she calmed a little.

Now we wait. The test results will be in tomorrow. Whatever it is, we will face it. I feel this girl deep in my heart, as I reflect on the different pet friends who have come and gone in my life. Taking root.

We are gifts to one another.

"No love, no friendship can cross the path of our destiny without leaving some mark on it forever."
— Francois Mauriac

HOMECOMING -
PENNY'S RETIREMENT

My bond with Penny runs deep. To the depth of my soul, I truly believe.

The look in her eyes indicates this nearly perfect golden retriever is approaching her golden years. She now relies upon me to do what is right for her. The signs have been there, I denied them. Penny has been a little less eager to put on her vest to go to the hospital, less interested in getting in and out of the car, and less enthusiastic about working with patients.

So this golden with her insatiable desire to bond and help humans is retiring from hospital pet therapy work. Oddly, it somehow helps for me to be able to write the words. I am hopeful that I may find another place for her talents that is less stressful for her and more fun, but in the meantime Miss Penny is ready for some greatly deserved R&R. She has done so much for so many since the day she was born that now it is her time.

For all of the patients who have grown to love her gentle nature and have had, if even for a moment, their pain alleviated by her presence, we will miss them, and we will always hold them close in our hearts and prayers.

For now I am ready for a homecoming for Penny and a celebration of her life by sharing her through this book.

And off stage is my very precocious two-year-old Petit Basset Griffon Vendeen (PBGV) eagerly learning the importance, challenge, and fun of being a pet therapy dog. Gracie (a French hound dog) is earning her own wings.

This 28-pound ball of energy was born with severe vision problems and has only about 10 percent sight.

From day one, Penny adopted Gracie as her own puppy and Gracie knew that Penny was her mom. This unlikely mother spent hours training Gracie. It was wonderful to watch as Penny would lead her around gently holding the puppy's ear between her teeth. She was truly Gracie's therapy dog, as well as her guide dog.

Remember—Penny, after two years of intense guide dog training, was released from the program. Looking back, this is what was supposed to happen. This golden ray of sunshine had a different assignment.

Through Penny's ministry, many of the lives she has touched will never be the same. I know mine won't and now through Gracie's contribution to the world of pet-assisted therapy, it will extend to literally hundreds of rehabilitation patients, family members, staff, and dog lovers everywhere. I was reminded of T. Seuss Geisel's wisdom when he said, "Don't cry because it's over. Smile because it happened."

Isn't it astonishing that two different species can work together for the good of both?

Penny and Gracie's personalities are different. Gracie is a comic genius!

She takes everything so very seriously, and I might say quite dramatically.

From her plush gray mouse squeaky toy, which is the joy of her life, to learning the world from sightless eyes, to joyfully leaping onto my lap each morning and turning upside down for a tummy rub, her approach to therapy work will be different, not in a bad way, just a different way.

Her enthusiasm is vastly amazing to watch. She enters the hospital gym by sound and smell. It is always the same. She stands on her little short stubby back legs, paws at the air with her front legs and dances in a circle while giving "the French hound dog is here" verbal "Arrrooo, Arrrooo" announcement.

The patients and staff return her greeting with applause and laughter. She will be a wonderful therapy dog. She, as did Penny, will change lives, alleviate pain, soften suffering, and inspire and challenge her patients to be the best that they can be.

Saving Gracie was one of the best things I ever did. Everyone told me not to adopt another dog, much less a blind puppy. "You need another dog like a hole in the head." "She will never be able to be a therapy dog."

But if I have learned nothing else in the past year, I have learned to pay attention to that "little voice." The universe was speaking, and I was stubborn. Although nobody wanted her, I knew that a visually-challenged puppy dog with great love and humor in her heart would be just what the doctor ordered. She has more than proved me correct.

Gracie has been working on a limited basis with patients at the rehab hospital for seven months on Sunday mornings. The staff lovingly call her "Sunday's child."

Great healing stories are anticipated once again…all from my saving Grace!

"Our pets lend a touch of grace to our lives. They teach us the real meaning of unconditional love and bring out the kindest and most generous impulses of humanity."

— Dr. Marty Becker
The Healing Power of Pets

My Broken Heart Has Healed

Medical science couldn't do it. Well-meaning friends had told me time would heal it. I wanted to hit them. Profound betrayal and mental abuse was a pain like none other I have ever known. It was accompanied by despair, irritability, restlessness, helplessness, emptiness, pessimism, and a complete lack of energy. I prayed constantly for strength, for grace, and for courage to get through another minute, another hour. Would the grief ever end from this broken heart?

Minute by minute I survived, minute by minute it was just a little easier, and minute by minute I became more acutely aware of the pain and sympathy of others struggling to survive. There are no quick fixes. It takes time and work. But just as I would not believe, nor expect, the pain did end.

I didn't know it at the time, but now I am aware of subtle messages that reached my heart and soul during the healing process.

I felt like I had lost everything that mattered most to me, but it was in losing that I found my dream. Through all the tears, and the sadness, and the pain, my passion has been revealed. How many people can say that they even know what their true passion is?

Now in my little corner of the world, my heart is at peace, and I feel intensely joyful. I am for the first time totally in love with life. For this I am enormously blessed.

One of Penny's patients called her "an angel." I smiled at Mazie as she watched Penny with such deep affection. Mazie was gazing deeply into Penny's soft brown eyes when she said, "You know, she may or may not be an angel, but her wings are there!" Very quietly, very peacefully and then very thoughtfully she said, "Penny is a glimpse into heaven."

Her wings are there. You only have to stop and look. If you lead from your heart and listen carefully, it will always be right. You, too, will find those subtle messages from the universe, whether from a brown-eyed golden retriever or another angel in disguise.

Be aware and experience the amazement.

The struggle to survive the pain allowed me to slow down to recognize the beauty around me. It became a time to care for my soul. A time to re-examine and re-evaluate my life and behavior patterns, and now I find that I am nicer to people and more in touch with things and people around me, life in general. It feels good. No, it feels great!

And through it all Penny has been there, teaching me about real love, the right kind, the peaceful kind. Teaching me that love should not hurt.

A Buddhist meditation says, "Start where you find yourself, then breathe." That's what I did. That's what Penny's patients do.

They move forward one step at a time. Identifying with another's journey is a first step toward compassion. And this compassion will bring great inner peace.

I always hold it close to my heart that these patients of Penny's have mothers, fathers, sisters, brothers, and maybe children and grandchildren. They are somebody's friend, mom, or dad. They, too, are in a relationship with the universe just as we are. This must not be forgotten.

My greatest hope is, if and when these people are at the end of their rope, Penny and I will be there to tie a knot into it and help them hold on. Much like my friends have done for me.

Pay it forward. Give the gift. Love is a healing thing. Healing sometimes is the ability not to fear. Healing sometimes is the ability to find life.

I have released the grief and am dearly holding onto what I have learned. I am living life with passion and listening to my heart.

There were times when Penny held one wing and I held the other, but I have found my wings. And my prayers have been answered.

> *"People who pray for courage, for strength to bear the unbearable, for the grace to remember what they have left instead of what they have lost, very often find their prayers answered. They discover that they have more strength, more courage than they ever knew themselves to have."*
>
> — Harold S. Kushner

THE HAPPY ENDING

I am frequently asked if *Penny's From Heaven* ends sadly.

Absolutely not! Penny is GREAT! Her test results indicated she is just fine. Rest assured, she will be well cared for the rest of her life.

Perhaps her symptoms could simply be, as always, my golden girl intuitively picking up on my stress, as she has done with hundreds of others.

She lies in the doorway of my office and occasionally comes to me and puts her head in my lap. I lay my hand on top of her head or her chest or side. I stop and focus and feel her heart beating and am, for that moment, again keenly aware of why I have written Penny's stories.

I feel I have written a pretty good book, not a perfect book, but a very honest book.

I don't know how this book got written, but I do know it was a gift. A gift to me that just maybe will make a difference in someone's life.

I have cried, and now I celebrate. It is the day before Easter. It is appropriate.

Be grateful for imperfect gifts.

"Normal day, let me be aware of the treasure you are. Let me learn from you, love you, bless you before you depart. Let me hold you while I may, for it may not always be so."

—Mary Jean Iron

"Just a Dog"

From time to time, people tell me, "lighten up, it's just a dog," or, "that's a lot of money for just a dog." They don't understand the distance traveled, the time spent, or the costs involved for "just a dog." Some of my proudest moments have come about with "just a dog." Many hours have passed and my only company was "just a dog," but I did not once feel slighted. Some of my saddest moments have been brought about by "just a dog," and in those days of darkness, the gentle touch of "just a dog" gave me comfort and reason to overcome the day.

If you, too, think it's "just a dog," then you will probably understand phases like "just a friend," "just a sunrise," or "just a promise." "Just a dog" brings into my life the very essence of friendship, trust, and pure unbridled joy. "Just a dog" brings out the compassion and patience that make me a better person.

Because of "just a dog" I will rise early, take long walks and look longingly to the future. So for me, and folks like me, it's not "just a dog" but an embodiment of all the hopes and dreams of the future, the fond memories of the past, and the pure joy of the moment. "Just a dog" brings out what's good in me and diverts my thoughts away from myself and the worries of the day.

I hope that someday they can understand that it's not "just a dog" but the thing that gives me humanity and keeps me from being "just a man." So the next time you hear the phrase "just a dog," just smile, because they "just don't understand."

- NAVHDA
- Richard Biby, Contributing Editor
- Broken Arrow, Oklahoma
Reprinted with permission

HEAVEN CAN WAIT

Well I must say, the world stopped when Penny walked into the rehab hospital after two months of retirement.

Penny's physical symptoms seem to have no apparent cause, so the consensus is that she is depressed. Could it be that this social golden-aged golden girl misses her friends, the adoration, and the attention—and most of all her job?

So to test this theory, I took her to RIOSA just for a quick little visit with "her friends."

The first stop was the recreation therapy room. Within seconds, faces lit up and most everyone got on the floor with her, brushed her, loved her, petted her, held her. The outpouring of emotion for Penny was overwhelming. I took lots of pictures with the staff lovin' on her. But I must say, the entire time I had a huge lump in my throat. Bittersweet!

Penny loved it. She would wag and then stand up and instantly plop down in someone's lap. Her favorite therapists were all but in tears at her return. It was amazing how much she has been missed and how deeply she is loved.

One of the male therapists mentioned a Mayberry television show where an old horse that had pulled the milk wagon around town had been retired. He stopped eating and acted strangely sad...until his owner realized he simply missed his job.

Guess that isn't too unlike many people. When long-awaited retirement finally comes, you feel lost, you miss your job, your friends; you have no real purpose any more.

So yes, once again Penny reminds us that just because we are a certain age, it doesn't mean we stop living. It doesn't mean we just have to sit around and do nothing. It means we have great wisdom to share. If Penny could speak, she would agree with Robert Frost. "I have promises to keep and miles to go before I sleep."

So I will find a purpose for Penny, and we will go visit her friends again soon. We will go to the fast food window and get a burger and "tots." We will walk and visit neighbors. And I will love her even more

As we prepared to leave RIOSA, each therapist told us good-bye and came up to me and told me to "take real good care of her because she is our dog, too."

I will.

"Don't cry because it is over. Smile because it happened."

T. Seusse Geisel

"If you want the things you love
You must have showers
So when you hear it thunder
Don't run under a tree
There'll be pennies from heaven
For you and me."

Music and Lyrics
by John Burke and Arthur Johnson

PRAISE FOR *PENNY'S FROM HEAVEN*

"I thoroughly enjoyed the stories, individually and as a collection. The messages were jet fuel for my spirit. I am far more likely to applaud/cheer in response to such events than to cry. It seems you wrote "Daily Meditations for the Therapeutic Animal Handler's Soul."
— Kris Butler, Author *Therapy Dogs Today: Their Gifts, Our Obligation* and *Therapy Dogs: Compassionate Modalities* (Book and DVD)

"A wonderful account of the power of four-legged love and its healing potential. These stories will touch your heart and nourish your soul. Enjoy."
— C. Collins "Andy" Anderson, DVM, MBA
Veterinary Surgeon, Diplomate ACVS
South Texas Veterinary Specialists, LLP

"To know the unconditional love and devotion of a dog is one of the greatest joys in life. It is no surprise that these delightful creatures provide such a potent healing force. Just stop and hug your dog, and you will feel the strength of the bond that exists between you and your best friend. *Penny's From Heaven* gives us insight into the wonderful relationship that exists between man and dog and reminds us of how important their medicine is to us."
— Greg Thompson, M.D.

"Of all God's creatures, golden retrievers are among my special favorites. Through her vital therapy work at the hospital, and now her stories, Penny shares her precious gifts and melts hearts, as well as barriers of trauma, age, loneliness, and recovery, with her bright-eyed golden smile—a true healing angel with four paws."
— Debra Baker, Co-Founder, Guide Dogs of Texas

"*Penny's From Heaven* is a wonderful celebration of the human-animal bond. The stories of healing and triumph amidst the background of despair and hardship will bring a tear to the reader's eye and a smile to the reader's heart. Your soul will be touched by the power in these seemingly small expressions of unconditional love toward those in need. We can learn much from Penny's simple tokens of grace. Thank you Patsy and Penny for sharing your ministry with us."

— Dan Earl, DVM
San Antonio, Texas, Penny's Doctor and Friend

"Humans, like our canine companions, are motivated by rewards. When our behavior achieves the desired result, we are rewarded. So, "heel" yourself to a bookstore, purchase *Penny's From Heaven*, then 'sit' in your favorite spot and 'read it.' Your reward...pure joy! This book is an awe-inspiring collection of how 'just a dog' can enrich the life of a human."

— Jasmine Skala, Dog Trainer and Behavior Counselor
Family Dog Obedience and the B.A.R.C. Club, San Antonio, TX

"*Penny's From Heaven* is full of wonderful stories that demonstrate the healing power of pets, both spiritually and physically, for people. Patsy is truly inspirational in her dedication and zeal to help people, utilizing pet therapy visitation and simple acts of compassion and empathy. Patsy shows how everyone can make a huge impact if they will put forth many small efforts. If you follow Patsy's example, you will be the beneficiary, as much as the recipient, of the power of the human-animal bond. Be prepared to cry and be inspired, all in one book."

— Jack L. Stephens, DVM
Founder, Pets Best-Health Insurance for Pets,
Skeeter Foundation, *Prescribe Pets, Not Pills*

"Penny has peace and understanding that most humans do not possess. Her intuitive and compassionate spirit aids patients in overcoming their disabilities to live independent, productive lives."

Aleen Davis Arabit, CEO
HEALTHSOUTH Rehabilitation Hospital
San Antonio, Texas

"Stroke rehabilitation is a multifaceted approach. Patsy and her remarkable therapy dog, Penny, provide our patients at HealthSouth Rehabilitation Institute of San Antonio with a very compassionate, nonjudgmental, and a warm modality for Neuro stimulation. Penny's visits with stroke survivors have shown to benefit both patient and therapists alike."

— Philip G. Onghai, M.D.
Neurology, Neurorehabilitation RIOSA
San Antonio, Texas

"These heartwarming stories of Penny portray the kindred spirits between patient and animal helping the other to survive and recover."

— Susan Hearn
Certified Therapeutic Recreation Specialist
HealthSouth RIOSA
San Antonio, Texas

"It has become well accepted that the soothing effect of a dog's visit exerts on patients has a beneficial response on their well being and enhances their recovery. This appears to be especially true among patients with coronary artery occlusive disease, where stress relief and lower blood pressure is most important. This is clearly demonstrated in the work Penny does at the rehab hospital and in her heartwarming stories."

— Dr. Leopoldo Zorrilla
Heart Surgeon, San Antonio, Texas

ABOUT THE AUTHOR

Patsy Swendson appeared on the CBS affiliate in South Texas for twenty years with her daily televised cooking program, worldwide travel features, and "Adopt a Pet" segments. She has authored 49 cookbooks. *Penny's From Heaven* is her first deviation from her culinary books.

Patsy produced and hosted a national award-winning five-part series called *Creature Comforts.* It focused on the human companion animal bond and pet-assisted therapy with children, the elderly, service dogs, therapy dogs, equine therapy, and even dolphin therapy. It was with this series that her passion began. *Creature Comforts* gained national attention with The Media Commendation Award from The Delta Society and The American Veterinary Medical Association's Mark Francis Award.

Patsy was featured in numerous magazines with her first therapy dog, Casey. She was a charter member of the San Antonio Delta Society chapter and became their second president, serving two terms. She was instrumental in getting the first legal health and temperament tested dogs in 68 health care facilities in South Texas and in forming the first Pet Loss Task Force in South Texas in conjunction with the United Way.

She began Operation Santa Paws where therapy dogs visited children, the elderly, and the needy each Christmas, beginning with The Blessing of the Delta Dogs on the San Antonio Riverwalk. And for her continuing support and understanding of the human companion-animal bond, she received The Lynn Anderson Distinguished Service Award in 1991.

For eight consecutive years, Patsy gave her full support to Guide Dogs of Texas with an annual benefit,

"The Patsy Swendson Unbirthday Bash and Barn Dance." It was their largest and most successful fund-raising event.

She served on the Board of Directors of the Bexar County Humane Society and was on the speaker's bureau for the American Heart Association and Stoke Survivors of San Antonio. She also hosted and produced a one-hour program, *Pet Pals*, focusing on human interest stories, lost and found pets, adopt a pet, veterinary medical discussions as well as controversial animal issues. This ran for one year and aired three times a week.

Patsy began "Ask the Vet," which was a weekly segment featuring local and national veterinarians discussing animal care and medicine. This segment ran for three years.

She produced and hosted a 30-minute documentary on animal abuse and pet overpopulation, called "What Are We Doing to Our Animals." This feature received much national attention.

Additionally, she produced and hosted another feature called "A Dog Named Charlie" about a dog nobody wanted and the ultimate fate.

Canine and Feline Cuisine: A Cookbook for Chewsy Pets was born out of her love of food and pets. The proceeds from this book were donated to Guide Dogs of Texas.

Patsy shares her home with Lulu, a 150-pound Great Pyrenees, Wally, a Lhaso apso rescue, Gracie Allen, a Petit Basset Griffon Vendeen rescue, Penny, a golden retriever, and Rita the turtle, an evacuee from Hurricane Rita.

PATSY SWENDSON HAS AUTHORED 49 COOKBOOKS.

Here are but a few.

Makin' Memories in the Kitchen (Eakin Publishing)
Popovers, Peaches and Four Poster Beds
    (Eakin Publishing)
Texas the Beautiful Cookbook (Harper Collins)
The Potluck Adventures of Mrs. Marmalade
    (Eakin Publishing)
Canine and Feline Cuisine: A Cookbook for Chew-sy
    Pets
Leona's Sanctuary – Recipes from Chimayo,
    New Mexico
Hill Country Mornings
San Antonio, Love at First Bite
Pralines, Pinatas and Peppers
Simply San Antonio
San Antonio the Lighter Side
Baked Alaska…and More
Solid Chocolate
Sweet Celebrations
Spa Cuisine
First You Make a Roux
Nutcracker Sweets
It's Better from Scratch I & II
Foods of the Mediterranean
Fit Recipes

TO ORDER COPIES
Penny's From Heaven

If this book is unavailable at your local bookstore,
LangMarc Publishing will fill your order
within 48 hours.

LangMarc Publishing
P.O. Box 90488 • Austin, Texas 78709-0488
Order on website: www.langmarc. com
or call 1-800-864-1648
or go to Patsy Swendson's site at
www.pennysfromheavenbook.com

Penny's From Heaven
Hardcover: $18.95 + $3.00 shipping • Priority: $4.50
(add $1 to shipping for each additional book)
Canada $24.95 + shipping

Please send payment with order:

_____ copies *Penny's From Heaven*   _____
8.25% Sales tax (Texas only)   _____
Shipping: _____

Amount of check enclosed: _____

Or your Credit card number and expiration date:
(MasterCard, Visa, or American Express)

_____

Expiration: _____

Name: _____

Address: _____

_____

Telephone number: _____